Belonging to
GOD

Belonging to
GOD

A PERSONAL TRAINING GUIDE
FOR THE DEEPER CATHOLIC
SPIRITUAL LIFE

Msgr. Charles M. Murphy

A Crossroad Book
The Crossroad Publishing Company
New York

The Crossroad Publishing Company
16 Penn Plaza, 481 Eighth Avenue
New York, NY 10001

Printed in the United States of America

Library of Congress Cataloging-in-Publication Data
Murphy, Charles M.
    Belonging to God : a personal training guide for the deeper
Catholic spiritual life / Charles M. Murphy.
        p.   cm.
    Includes bibliographical references.
    ISBN 0-8245-2148-X (alk. paper)
    1. Spiritual life – Catholic Church.   I. Title.
BX2350.3.M87 2004
248.4'82 – dc22
                                        2003026595

1   2   3   4   5   6   7   8   9   10   10   09   08   07   06   05   04

For Sheila

Contents

Foreword

The need of a *Regula Vitae* (Rule of Life) for the Catholic laity has been clear for at least two centuries. Priests and those in consecrated life abound in rich, spiritual advice. But the vocation and mission of the laity differ from those of the ordained and religious. The rule of life for a cloistered St. Thérèse of Lisieux in her Carmel convent could not have been effective for her sainted parents, Louie and Zélie Martin, in their daily work and family life. And the Martins of our time have little practical direction on how to live a holy life in a postmodern world. As president of the Pontifical Council for the Laity for seven years, I was acutely aware of this lack.

What would a *Regula Vitae* of the laity look like? What particulars would it include? Pope John Paul II has a comprehensive vision. He defined "spirituality" in general as "a mode or form of life in keeping with Christian demands" (*Ecclesia in America*, 29). A lay spirituality would give particular form to their "secular" vocation, i.e., the call to holiness in the world, guided by the Holy Spirit. *Belonging to God* is a useful and needed contribution in assisting the lay baptized in their response to the call to holiness while making a living in the marketplace.

The book's title was used by Pope John Paul II in his 2001 Apostolic Letter *Novo Millennio Ineunte* to describe the Church's holiness: "The rediscovery of the Church as 'mystery'...was bound to bring with it a rediscovery of the Church's holiness, understood in the basic sense of belonging to him who is in essence

the Holy One, the 'thrice Holy'" (30). In choosing his title Monsignor Murphy has made clear the bond between holiness and a
lay *Regula Vitae*.

Although drawing upon the spiritual and theological treasures
of the major spiritual traditions within the Catholic Church, Monsignor Murphy gives priority to the Salesian School, founded by
St. Francis de Sales (1567–1622) and St. Jane Frances de Chantal (1572–1641). In *Belonging to God* St. Francis is consistently
referred to as "St. Francois." It is a happy choice, for it immediately distinguishes St. Francis de Sales from the founder of another
great tradition of sanctity within the Church, Francis of Assisi.

The book's reliance upon St. Francois and St. Jane is fitting
since the bishop of Annecy and the foundress of the Order of the
Visitation both matured in an era, the early Baroque, which bears
striking similarities to our own. In fact, it gave birth to modern
times. The two saints lived and matured amid an enormous cultural crisis. One recalls the amazement caused by the scientific
discoveries of Kepler and Galileo, who were their contemporaries,
and of Nicholas Copernicus, who died some years earlier.

The experiences of men and women of the early years of the
Baroque are akin to our own. They knew something of our un-
certainties, our awareness of the limits of existence before the
expansiveness of the universe, our interior torments, our wonder
and struggle before Blaise Pascal's two infinities: space and the
tiny particles undergirding nature. In a later Baroque era, during the 1660s, that French Catholic layman wrote, "For who will
not be astounded at the fact that our body, itself imperceptible in
the universe, . . . is now a colossus, a world, or rather a whole in
respect of the nothingness which we cannot reach. He who re-
gards himself in this light will be afraid of himself, and observing
himself sustained in the body given him by nature between those
two abysses of the Infinite and Nothing, will tremble at the sight

of these marvels, and I think that, as his curiosity changes into admiration, he will be more disposed to contemplate them in silence than to examine them with presumption." In the twenty-first century who can fail to identify with Pascal's reverential silence?

The two founders of the Salesian School shared the amazement of their contemporaries before the newly discovered immensity of the universe. In responding to the cultural upheaval of the Baroque era, St. Francois drew upon some of the leaders of the Spanish School who immediately preceded him: St. John of the Cross, Luis of Granada, and, above all, St. Teresa of Avila. In a more direct fashion, *Belonging to God* is a continuing dialogue within the ancient spiritual tradition of the Catholic Church — with St. Francois and, to a lesser extent, with St. Jane and, more remotely, with St. Augustine of Hippo. Writing in an Augustinian narrative style, Monsignor Murphy makes readily accessible the ancient Christian wisdom to modern readers.

St. Francois possessed a pastoral passion to show the laity the way of holiness. *Belonging to God* captures his passion. Monsignor Murphy frequently and aptly draws upon examples from numerous saints and from his own pastoral experience to illustrate the five Salesian spiritual principles. Moreover, we find here all the main Salesian themes: listening to the heart, commitment, perfect freedom, joy in belonging to God, the importance of ordinary things — all founded upon and enhanced by the "little" virtues. Using one of his ubiquitous and happy illustrations, St. Francois describes the "little" virtues as the practice of "those ordinary virtues suited to our littleness . . . which are better practiced in going downhill than in climbing and suit our legs better: patience, forbearance toward our neighbor, service to others, humility, gentleness of heart, affability, tolerance of our own imperfections, and similar little virtues." *Belonging to God* reintroduces the Catholic laity to an ancient moral theology based on the virtues in which attention to human happiness or beatitude, interior acts, and finality predominate.

There is a less explicit but no less important lesson in *Belonging to God*. By elaborating on the "Christian friendship" of the two Baroque saints in chapter 7, Monsignor Murphy considers one of the most controverted issues in Church and society, the relation of man and woman.

The creative complementarity of a man and a woman in the founding of the Salesian School remains a historic example of the extraordinary teaching of Pope John Paul II in *Christifideles Laici The Lay Members of Christ's Faithful People*, 52): "[There is] an urgent need for every Christian to live and proclaim the message of hope contained in the relation between man and woman. The Sacrament of Matrimony, which consecrates this relation in its conjugal form and reveals it as a sign of the relation of Christ with his Church, contains a teaching of great importance for the Church's life — a teaching that ought to reach today's world through the Church; *all those relations between man and woman must be imbued by this spirit*" (italics mine). The spiritual friendship of St. Francois and St. Jane, spanning nineteen years, is a classic realization of the pope's vision.

Along the same line, Wendy Wright and Joseph F. Power, O.S.F.S., comment on the significance of the relationship between the two saints for our time: "Their own ardent and poignant bond . . . drew them together into a mature love of God. It was precisely in the midst of that friendship with all the powerful dynamics between male and female that they both learned what it was to make Jesus live fully. And they extended themselves in friendship to a wide circle of intimates giving credence to the Pauline assertion that friendship is the bond of perfection."

According to St. Francois there is also an inviolable condition for moving toward the perfect freedom of husband and wife. In affirming the overarching importance of the virtues of chastity, modesty, and purity in marriage, he insists in a particular manner that the holiness of man and woman in marriage is dependent upon the ancient teachings of the Church on the sanctity of the conjugal union. Pope Paul VI and Pope John Paul II have frequently insisted upon the respect of all peoples for the nature and finality of the conjugal act. St. Francois founded the holiness of marriage on this teaching (*Introduction* 3, XXXIX) and considered the fruitfulness of conjugal love an intrinsic foundation of holiness in the married state. Msgr. Murphy states this specifically when he writes, "The first and principal purpose of sexual relations is to produce children."

In 1968 Pope Paul VI reaffirmed this ancient Christian teaching: "It is necessary that each and every marriage act must remain open to the transmission of life" (*Humanae Vitae* 11). Further on the pope continues, "The direct interruption of the generative process already begun must be totally rejected as a legitimate means of regulating the number of children" (*Humanae Vitae* 14). He called such a rejection a characteristic of "responsible parenthood."

The Pastoral Constitution on the Church in the Modern World of the Second Vatican Council (37) gives a succinct description of the virtues needed by Christians engaged in secular life and culture. By doing so the Council emphasizes a fundamental theme of the Salesian School and of *Belonging to God*, the role of virtues in Christian life. Virtuous Christians represent something totally new in the world. They are a new creation. They are brothers and sisters of the one "designated Son of God in power according to the Spirit of holiness by his resurrection from the dead, Jesus Christ our Lord" (Rom. 1:4). According to the Council, the lay baptized in Christ Jesus can and must love the things which God has created. They receive them, guard them, and honor them as they have come forth from God's hands. But lay Christians should be "using and enjoying creation in poverty and freedom. In so doing [each person] comes into the possession of the world as if possessing nothing and yet possessing all things (2 Cor. 6:10ff.) — 'all things are yours, but you are Christ's and Christ is of God.' "

That word, "enjoying" (*fruens* in Latin), joined with the other classic word "using" (*utens* in Latin), opens lay Christians to a morality of virtues. The way of holiness is no longer characterized by a prevailing flight and horror of the world, but by a responsibility in and for the world. The holiness of the lay baptized is based on the *prudent* "enjoyment" and "use" of the things of this world in poverty and liberty of spirit. Those two Latin words, *fruens* and *utens*, capture the teaching of the Second Vatican Council concerning the prudence characteristic of the holiness of the laity — a teaching reflected in *Belonging to God.*

It is evident that *Belonging to God* is more than a simple repetition of the principles of the Salesian School of holiness for those making a living in the world. The elaboration on the Salesian "little" virtues draws inspiration from the teachings of the Second Vatican Council and the postconciliar magisterium. Monsignor Murphy indicates that it is not an accident of history that Blessed Pope John XXIII, the father of the Second Vatican Council, was personally formed by the Salesian School. In his *Journal of a Soul,* Blessed John acknowledges his indebtedness: "I must desire, not to be what I am not, but to be very truly what I really am. That is what my St. Francois de Sales tells me."

Belonging to God gives the *Christifideles Laici* an exquisite, contemporary *Regula Vitae.*

J. Francis Cardinal Stafford
Major Penitentiary
Solemnity of All Saints, 2003

Belonging to
GOD

Introduction

Becoming a Spiritual Person

In my work as a priest, I have met many people who truly believe themselves to be spiritual. By this they mean that they have a basic belief in God and are convinced that their life holds a deeper meaning than simply going through the motions every day. At some point they may desire to explore the spiritual side of their lives more seriously. To do this, they may seek the help of a spiritual guide or director.

Within the Catholic tradition, a spiritual director is an important resource. He or she is like a personal trainer for the spirit. To maintain good physical fitness, it is helpful to engage a personal trainer. A personal trainer helps us to achieve our goals for fitness by laying out a program that will get us where we want to be without harming ourselves. A personal trainer also provides encouragement, support, motivation, and, sometimes, the correction and challenge we need if we are to make progress and not regress. The same is true in the spiritual realm.

This book is intended as a personal training guide for beginners in the spiritual life who do not have the luxury of a personal spiritual director. It is also designed to help people new or old in their faith to establish basic and sound structures and practices that will give shape to their spiritual lives.

Belonging to God grew out of a series of spiritual direction sessions I conducted with one young man in my parish. I met Steve when he and his wife, Margarete, asked to have their child baptized. Easter was approaching, the feast in which Baptism is most appropriately celebrated. I suggested that Keller's Baptism take place at the great Easter Vigil when several people, young and old, who had been in preparation for many months, would be received into the Church and would be given new life in Christ. The Easter Vigil, the solemn liturgy of waiting in the night for Christ's glorious Resurrection, is the most impressive celebration in the entire Christian year. Adults who have been in the Christian Initiation process and infants like Keller are baptized in the Easter water of rebirth. During the Vigil, the adults also receive the sacraments of Confirmation and Holy Eucharist to complete their initiation. For infants like Keller, these sacraments will come later.

Plans were set for the Baptism, but Steve had an additional request, an unusual one: he wanted to be baptized at the same time. Married to a Catholic, he wished deeply to join his daughter at the baptismal font. I hesitated. Steve had not undergone the extensive preparation required for this major step. As we met together to discuss his request, I came to appreciate how Steve's whole spiritual search until now had resulted in his fervent desire to be baptized. I discovered that he already possessed the basic gift, the gift of faith, which would qualify him for Baptism. That gift, which had saved him from several potentially destructive experiences in the past, only needed to be enhanced by greater knowledge and grounding in the Church's traditions and beliefs. I agreed to baptize him, with the condition that he meet with me weekly afterward to fill in the blanks.

Steve later presented me with a picture of himself and his daughter, both in their white baptismal robes, and of his wife standing with them. Steve said he was "blown away" by the whole experience of the Easter Vigil and its powerful symbols of light shining in the darkness, the water of rebirth, the bread, and the wine.

Candidates who are baptized at Easter continue their process of initiation for a time after Easter in a period called *mystagogia*, a Greek term that means "reflecting upon the mysteries." "Mysteries" is the Greek-derived word for the Latin "sacraments." In the weeks after Easter the newly baptized and confirmed try to appreciate and grasp more fully the graces that have been so abundantly given to them in these two sacraments and in the greatest sacrament of all, the Holy Eucharist of Christ's own Body and Blood communicated to them.

St. Francois's method is for lay-people who do not have the luxury to spend hours in prayer and meditation.

Sometimes the *mystagogia* is described as the weakest phase of the Christian Initiation process. After the initial enthusiasm, in this phase some fall away, lacking the supports and structures that guided them into reception into the Church. *Belonging to God* is intended to help such people to continue to grow in faith. It is also designed to help people like Steve who need to give shape to their spiritual lives if they are to continue to develop and deepen the gift they have received, the gift of wanting to become a spiritual person.

A Method

Every competent personal trainer follows a philosophy and method. The theory and method that *Belonging to God* is based on have proven themselves through positive results in many people's lives over the past several centuries. The method is laid out in a classic work of spirituality, *Introduction to the Devout Life*, written by a saint and doctor (holy teacher) of the Church, St. Francois de Sales (1567–1622). St. Francois is often referred to outside his native France as St. Francis, but I prefer to call him by the name he was given rather than anglicizing it. His book also grew out of spiritual direction sessions with a layperson who had turned to him for help. Earlier, St. Francois had encountered a young widow in spiritual crisis, Baroness Jeanne-Francoise de Chantal (1572–1641). Jeanne-Francoise not only became someone he counseled, but also herself contributed greatly to his spiritual teaching. St. Francois's method is for laypeople who do not have the luxury to spend hours in prayer and meditation as would cloistered monks and nuns in a monastery. It is based upon the conviction, in St. Francois's own words, that "it is an error, or, rather, a heresy, to wish to banish the devout life from the regiment of soldiers, the mechanic's shop, the court of princes, or the home of married people."[1] It is for people who have to make a living in this world.

According to St. Francois, we do not need to make radical changes in our daily routines because our spiritual life is not a special time set aside from our daily life: it *is* our daily life lived in a certain way. Our spiritual life is simply doing all we do out of the love of God.[2]

St. Francois was a "montagnard," a man of the mountains, from the Savoie region of France, near Switzerland. His spirituality is filled with charming allusions to the natural world in which he lived and from which he drew spiritual strength. His spiritual method, he says, is to do no harm, like bees that draw nectar from flowers without hurting them, leaving them as whole and fresh as they were found. "True devotion," which is his phrase for the spiritual method he taught, "not only does not do injury to one's vocation or occupation but on the contrary adorns and beautifies it."[3]

So many spiritualities that we are offered today are, by comparison, a thin broth distilled from a variety of ingredients: psychology, Eastern mysticism, New Age notions, meditation techniques, and physical and dietary regimes. The method of St. Francois de Sales is solidly Christian and eminently flexible and practical. It can shape a spiritual life into a path to holiness.

We Are All Called to Be Holy

One of the greatest contributions of the Second Vatican Council (1962–65) was to address the spiritual life of laypeople. The Council taught that everyone, clergy and laity, is called to holiness, the same perfection, but by different paths: Everyone without exception is called to be holy.[4] The teaching of St. Francois in many ways anticipated the Council and provides a way to put its teachings into practice.

But what does it mean to become holy? Does it mean being "extra good"? Doing exceptional, heroic deeds? Being burned at the stake, a martyr for the faith? If so, few people would feel called to such holiness. No, to be holy is to discover and to accept that we belong to God, who alone is holy.

All of us try, in one way or another, to find our place in the world. The process of finding this out is often by trial and error. We've reached our destination when we discover that ultimately we belong to no one except to God. God made us, and only God can satisfy the deepest longings of our hearts. When we know this, we are on the road to holiness.

When someone is consecrated to God, like a monk or nun, or when an object, like a chalice or sacred vestment, is blessed to be used only for the worship of God, that person or object is said to be "holy." They have been set aside for God. This does not mean necessarily that they are "good" in the moral sense but that they now belong only to God.[5] So, too, with us.

The sacraments of Baptism, Confirmation, and Holy Eucharist make us God's own, brothers and sisters of Jesus. The spiritual method of St. Francois is intended to help us own and develop our divine status as holy people belonging to God. Some, St. Francois says, imagine devout people "as having discontented, gloomy, sullen faces," or claim "that devotion brings on depression and unbearable moods." He says, "On the contrary, the devout life is a life that is sweet, happy, and lovable."[6] This life is so congenial because it is a life that fits us.

This method is very different from a self-help program based only on our efforts. Such programs have only temporary effects because by ourselves we are extremely limited. A Christian spiritual method, on the other hand, is based on God's grace.

For example, when we are initially called by God to be his own through the sacrament of Baptism, it is not from any special worthiness or previous accomplishments on our part. It is a gift freely and generously given. Even infants who are helpless and as yet incapable of faith can truly become God's own in Baptism, his own sons and daughters and sharers in the divine nature.

When we later strive to complete the holiness we have received by practicing a virtuous life, we are able to do so only with the assistance of grace. This path to holiness is quite different from a kind of perfectionism by which we would aim for a standard that is inhuman in its demands. According to the Second Vatican Council, the "perfection of charity" that is the goal of the Christian life is something eminently human and accessible to people in all walks of life.[7]

Given our different circumstances, every person's path to holiness will be somewhat different. For this reason, the method of St. Francois is extremely flexible. He said,

Devotion must be exercised in different ways by the gentleman, the worker, the servant, the prince, the widow, the young girl, and the married woman. Not only is this true, but the practice of devotion must be adapted to the strength, activities, and duties of each particular person. I ask you . . . is it fitting for a bishop to want to live a solitary life like a Carthusian? Or for married men to want to own no more property than a Capuchin, for a skilled workman to spend the whole day in church like a religious, for a religious to be constantly subject to every sort of call in his neighbor's service, as a bishop is? Would not such devotion be laughable, confused, impossible to carry out?[8]

For example, St. Francois's program calls for an absolute minimum of one hour of meditation a day. In meditation we begin to "learn" Jesus, his ways of thinking and acting. Ideally this meditation hour should take place soon after rising in the morning. This gives us a spiritual perspective at the start of each day and a sense of peace that we can return to in the midst of the day's activities. But if you told St. Francois, "I don't have an hour to meditate," he would reply, "All right, how much time do you have? Ten minutes? I'll take ten minutes, but do it every day." Can't fit in meditation early in the morning? "All right, do it when you can, but do it. Persistent effort is what counts."

Practicing Holiness

It may seem strange and even inappropriate to speak of holiness as something you can practice. But holiness — which Pope John Paul II also defines, as we have, as "belonging to God"[9] — is a divine gift that brings with it a human task. Our Christian faith as described in the Acts of the Apostles is not only a doctrine but a "way," a new way of walking in this world (Acts 9:2). Jesus described himself as our "way, truth, and life" (John 14:6). Holiness then is something we are to practice every day. I love the response one man gave when asked what kind of Catholic he was. He replied, "I'm a practicing Catholic. That is to say, I'm not perfect, so I have to keep practicing."

I have distilled the spiritual teachings of St. Francois into five principles for daily living, the beginning of a method whose ultimate goal is falling in love with God. When we finally decide to love God with our whole heart, soul, and mind, and to love our neighbor as ourselves (Mark 12:30), we have embarked upon what St. Francois de Sales calls "devotion." It is the moment when "charity bursts into flames."[10]

Part One

SPIRITUALITY

One

Five Spiritual Principles for Beginners

Our spiritual life begins when we become aware, in a personal revelation, that we are truly loved by God. When I met Steve he had been married twice and had three children, two sons from his first marriage and a daughter from his present one. It was through the birth of his baby daughter, Keller, with whom he was baptized at Easter, that Steve became aware again of God's unconditional love for him. Steve's day usually begins with playtime with Keller. "When I walk into her room," he explains, "she lights up and rushes toward me, sometimes falling in her excitement to greet me and picking herself up." Steve gave me a photograph of himself and Keller taken the night of their Baptism. In it father and daughter are garbed in their white baptismal robes, designating them as newborn children of God. Steve recognizes their love for each other as God's gift and a window into the immensity of God's love for them both.

Steve feels blessed also in the love of his wife, whose talents as a social worker and counselor have brought so much to his own life. He also takes special pride in his two sons — one doing well in college, majoring in literature and exploring his own talents for poetry, the other still in high school and a star athlete excelling in three sports. Steve says, "They give me my purpose in life. I see myself in them and I am proud."

But the formative experience of God that Steve will never forget came at a time in his life when everything seemed black. He was nineteen. His glory years as part of the state championship baseball team were over. He was working for his stepfather — a stern taskmaster — in the construction business. His stepfather was injured and was bedridden for five years. Before Steve could handle such responsibilities, he was given full charge of the business and all its employees. It was too much.

One night at about ten o'clock he was lying in bed, sleepless. All his worries were keeping him awake. A light pierced the darkness of his room. It came through a window and played on the ceiling. He felt himself in the presence of an angel who brought great comfort. Steve was filled with awareness. He seemed to be given knowledge of what life would bring him and that his future was in safe hands. As the sense of the angel's presence departed, he was left with a feeling of being blessed. Steve had experienced a powerful revelation of God's love for him.

From that moment on, Steve felt a new confidence in himself. His mind was at peace and his life took on a new direction. Soon he met the woman he would marry, and their two sons were born. Time passed and the angel's message faded from Steve's mind. He was too preoccupied with a whole new set of responsibilities to pay attention to his heart and its needs. As working parents with two young children, the young couple faced mounting pressures, which eventually became too much. Arguments started about who was supposed to do what; both Steve and his wife felt overextended and unappreciated. They developed a pattern of heavy drinking to handle their stress. In the end they divorced.

By the time I met Steve, he had already begun his discovery of the basic principles of the spiritual life. He had learned them from his own need to survive. Through his participation in alcoholic rehabilitation, he became aware of the need to listen to himself better. For example, if he attended properly to it, his body would tell him when to rest and when to eat. He discovered what gave him the greatest pleasure and what nourished his spirit; it had to do with building things. By artfully arranging stone upon stone something practical as well as beautiful came into being by his own hands. Gazing upon what he had done gave him great happiness. Stonemasonry was something he was good at, and he delighted in it.

Other important insights came when Steve's employment ended and he needed to find another job. For men, employment is often their identity, the badge of their worth as people. For a man to find himself without a job is to be particularly vulnerable. With Margarete's encouragement, Steve didn't simply leap into the first employment opportunity that came along. Instead, he attended a seminar for people between jobs; it was called "A New Path." Rather than making the job with the highest paycheck his goal, Steve was taught to step back and consider such deep, hard questions as, "What is your passion? What would you truly like to do if you were given the chance? What do you think your true vocation in life is?"

At the same time, Steve and I began to meet. Steve was able to reconnect with his feelings about God, a missing piece in his life until then. He recalled the angel's visitation he had received so many years before. God was in his heart and so his heart would not lead him astray. Steve's life began to change. He no longer felt the need to go out and party as he once did; he was content staying at home, getting a good night's sleep, and keeping a human pace. Enjoying the company of his daughter was enough. Playing sports and coaching his son's team, he came to see, were not just optional leisure-time events but sources of great satisfaction as well as good ways of handling life's ordinary stress. Steve was formulating, without using this terminology, the basic principles of a spiritual life for himself.

The Spirituality of St. Francois de Sales

The spirituality of St. Francois and St. Francois himself are one and the same. It has been said of him that "he was the freshest, freest, easiest of the great saints — and the most humanly attractive."[1] None of these qualities came to him naturally: they were the results of his hard spiritual work. It was only after dead ends and disastrous events that St. Francois came to accept his own humanity. It was one of his most significant spiritual breakthroughs.

Two events particularly shaped St. Francois and his spirituality. As a teenager in Paris he succumbed to a profound depression that lasted nearly two weeks. There were physical symptoms, but talking about it later, St. Francois described it as a spiritual crisis. He was convinced that he was predestined to go to hell and could do nothing about it. He prayed to God, asking to be allowed to love God, even in hell. The depression lifted when he wandered into a chapel, knelt before an image of Mary, the Mother of God, and picked up a board that had the following prayer written on it:

> Remember, O most gracious Virgin Mary, that never was it known that anyone who fled to your protection, implored your help, or sought your intercession, was left unaided. Inspired by this confidence, I fly unto you, O Virgin of Virgins, my Mother. To you I come; before you I stand sinful and sorrowful. O Mother of the Word Incarnate! Despise not my petitions but in your mercy hear and answer me. Amen.

This prayer, called the "Memorare" from its Latin original, communicated to the young St. Francois the maternal love of Mary, who embraced him in spite of — or more accurately, in terms of his new spiritual insight, *because* of — his humanity.

The other incident occurred in law school. His father, who was a domineering figure in his life, had determined that Francois would be a lawyer. After college he went from Paris to Padua, the Italian city with the most famous law faculty in the world. Francois was strictly supervised by a chaplain in his father's employ. While there, St. Francois continued to take self-discipline to excess in his attempts to become "holy." He punished himself with the most rigorous penances and extended prayers, to the point that he nearly died.

This crisis in Padua was far more serious than the earlier one in Paris. It had two major components, one intellectual, the other moral. His intellect struggled with whether he should set aside his own notions of right and wrong, as well as his life experience, and embrace what he was taught — that our human nature is basically corrupt and that, regardless of personal merit, God predestines people to either heaven or hell.

The moral problem came from the spirituality of the time, which taught that body and soul are enemies of one another and that the body must be brought under the soul's control through rigorous penance and acts of will. St. Francois felt that only his own pride kept him from accepting the teachings of the Church. He blamed his human nature for his failure to achieve moral perfection.

In the end, he survived because he came to accept what his own mind and heart told him: that he was all right and that everything would be all right because human nature is good, not bad, and because God is love. He could hope again.

Having survived this crisis he faced another back at home after his graduation from law school: his father's plans. Francois returned to the Savoie to discover that his father had selected a woman for him to marry. His experiences of misery in Paris and Padua had taught St. Francois that, for the sake of his own survival, he had to pay attention to his heart and to be gentle with his spirit. He asked his mother to break the news to his father that he was not going to practice law and was not getting married: he was going to become a priest.

"A saint who is sad is a sad saint indeed."

Ste. Jeanne-Francoise said later that what struck her most about her spiritual director was how unexceptional he was. "He kept to the common way but in a manner so divine and heavenly that this was, as I see it, the most wonderful thing about his life."[2] The man she knew had at long last rid himself of all his burdens, self-imposed and otherwise, and was free to be himself.

It becomes completely understandable in this light that St. François's entire spirituality is based upon this text from the Gospel according to St. Matthew, his favorite in all the Bible:

> Come to me, all you who labor and are overburdened, and I will give you rest. Shoulder my yoke and learn from me, for I am gentle and humble in heart, and you will find rest for your souls. Yes, my yoke is easy and my burden light.
>
> (Matt. 11:28–30)

Henri Brémond, an historian of French spirituality, describes the fundamental aspect of St. Francois's spirituality as devout humanism. Salesian spirituality is certainly about being devout and committed, but it is always respectful of our humanity.[3] Speaking about himself, St. Francois willingly admitted, "I am as human as anyone could possibly be."[4] He counseled those who would strive to be saints at the expense of being human, "First try to be a good enough human being.... Sometimes it happens that those who imagine themselves angels are not even good at being human."[5] It is better to start by trying to be pleasant to live with. In one of his most memorable aphorisms, St. Francois quipped, "A saint who is sad is a sad saint indeed."[6]

St. Francois's spirituality has the humble goal of wishing only to adorn and beautify our lives. One word that recurs in his spirituality is *douceur,* which literally means "sweetness." *Douceur* evokes a distant age when gentlemen and ladies exercised *politesse,* cultivating good manners and civilized conversations, and never knowingly giving offense. But *douceur* also discloses a high moral ideal — of maintaining an imperturbable calm whatever the circumstances and making it seem easy. The English Benedictine monk Dom Bernard Mackey, O.S.B., who edited the voluminous writings of St. Francois, carried away the impression that St. Francois made the spiritual life "secure, easy, and sweet."[7]

The Five Spiritual Principles

To set ourselves upon a safe spiritual path, one that will build upon our humanity and not burden it, the following are the sound spiritual principles that will stand us in good stead for the long haul.

1. Listen deeply to your heart and trust what it says.

2. Commit your heart firmly to God.

3. Strive gently for perfect freedom of heart.

4. Belong joyfully to God in the midst of all you do.

5. Do each day's ordinary things with great love.

1. Listen Deeply to Your Heart and Trust What It Says

There are lots of reasons why, like St. Francois, we may never have attended to our own hearts or even thought it a good idea to do so. Most often people have to follow the "exterior agenda," those obligations and expectations that we learn to live with and feel no power to change. From the time we get up in the morning until the time we go to bed, our entire day has usually been programmed for us. Furthermore, listening to our own hearts may strike us as profoundly selfish and not at all virtuous.

But the cost of not attending to our hearts is high. Until our health suffers or we develop destructive life patterns, we may not realize that our spirits are bruised and battered and we may not even recognize ourselves anymore.

Christian theology might seem to imply that listening to our unredeemed hearts could lead us astray. Ever since the fall of our first parents our hearts have become distorted by the milieu of sin in which we live. But Christian theology also teaches that even though the image of God has become tarnished within us, our hearts have never lost their fundamental attraction toward God. If we listen deeply enough to what our heart says, we will hear God speaking. The problem comes if we do not listen deeply enough and we mistake superficial and selfish desires for what our hearts really want.

In St. Francois's other masterpiece, the *Treatise on the Love of God*, he sets forth why he believes we can trust our own hearts.

And although now our human nature be not endowed with that original soundness and righteousness which the first man had in his creation, but on the contrary be greatly depraved by sin, yet still the holy inclination to love God above all things stays with us, as also the natural light by which we see his sovereign goodness to be more worthy of love than all things; and it is impossible that one thinking attentively upon God, yes even by natural reasoning only, should not feel a certain movement of love which the secret inclination of our nature excites in the bottom of our hearts.... It is the same ... with our heart, which though it be formed, nourished, and bred amongst corporal, base, and transitory things, and in the manner under the wings of nature, notwithstanding, at the first look it throws on God, at its first knowledge of him, the natural and first inclination to love God which was dull and imperceptible, awakes in an instant, and suddenly appears as a spark from amongst the ashes, which touching our will gives it a movement of the supreme love due to the sovereign and first principle of all things.[8]

St. Francois lived at a time when there was a great distrust of human instinct and a profound awareness of how easily corruptible human nature has become. We have already seen how as a teenager St. Francois became convinced that he was an irremediable sinner. Discovering natural goodness in himself came as a liberation and a reason to hope once more. Neither are we doomed to a life of frustration or dreary duty because God "is the God of my heart," the source of its greatest pleasure and delight, as St. Augustine taught in his *Confessions.*[9]

St. Francois is not credited with being an innovative thinker. Much of his spiritual writings is derived from masters like St. Augustine. Cardinal Henri de Lubac, S.J., a leading modern theologian, points out, however, how novel and refreshing St. Francois was in his own age in insisting that it was safe to trust your heart.[10] The New Law of Jesus, we are told, is "written upon our hearts" (Heb. 8:10). It is there that the Holy Spirit dwells. If we attend to the Spirit's voice, the Spirit will lead us into all truth (John 14:26). We will know the truth, and the truth will set us free (John 8:32).

2. Commit Your Heart Firmly to God

The spiritual path we have adopted for ourselves has been accurately defined as "devout humanism." It has also been called "inspired common sense." Motivated by the love of God, it makes even the most difficult tasks "pleasant, sweet, and easy."[11] It would be a serious misreading to suggest that this spirituality is not challenging and rigorous. The role of the will is huge, and great emphasis is placed upon making firm resolutions. The first requirement of committing our hearts to God is that we not only liberate ourselves from sinful patterns but also from any desire to return to them.[12] Prayer, so central to this spirituality, is never just whiling away time with Jesus but "learning" Jesus so that we can commit ourselves to his way of thinking and acting with greater and greater fidelity. Every meditation has a bottom line: what new resolutions am I to take from this prayer that will affect how I live? It rules out self-complacency[13] and fulfills the requirement laid down by Pope John Paul II that we not settle for spiritual mediocrity and shallowness.

St. Francois confronts us with stark choices. We have only one life to live; in life there are no dress rehearsals. We are accountable for ourselves not only to ourselves and others but to God. St. Francois is graphic in describing the eternal repercussions of the way we choose to live; heaven or hell will be our final destiny. God is love, but the choice is ours whether to accept or reject it. "I accept the offer you are pleased to give me," St. Francois says we are to pray. "O Jesus my Savior, I accept your everlasting love."[14]

This spirituality is all about love — being loved and loving in return. But like all love, if it is real and is to last it has to have a spine: the firm commitment of the will in holy, life-changing resolutions. When St. Augustine first called the commitment of the will central to the meaning of love, he gave it a new and specifically Christian substance. Love is more than a feeling, in other words. Feelings come and go; love, it if is a commitment, remains.

We should be clear that the crucial role of the will in committing the heart to God does not reduce the spiritual life to "will power" triumphing over human desire. By clearing away sinful desires we discover where our truest and deepest desires really are and how to fulfill them. We discover the desire to do God's will. To want to do the will of God will above all else leads to the greatest fulfillment and personal nourishment. "This is my food," Jesus said of himself, "to do the will of the one who sent me" (John 4:34).

3. Strive Gently for Perfect Freedom of Heart

Choices involve losses as well as gains — we always choose one thing over another. If our ultimate choice is doing God's will, then we will have to let go of everything that gets in its way. God's will for us, as we have seen, is perfect freedom. Letting go of anything that threatens to possess us is part of entering into God's freedom.

Among the paths to blessedness announced by Jesus in his Beatitudes is what St. Matthew calls "poverty of spirit." For St. Luke, it was simply "poverty." A person who is literally poor and dependent upon others is already in the right spiritual posture in regard to God; the illusion of independence and self-sufficiency that wealth brings has been stripped away. St. Matthew qualified the beatitude as "poverty of spirit": we all have possessions, he implies; how we relate to them determines our spiritual condition.

Following this line of thought, St. Francois asks who possesses whom? Do our possessions possess us or are we sufficiently de-tached from them that their loss would not be a catastrophe?[15] "Your heart," he says, "must be open to heaven alone."[16]

In our sessions together, Steven admitted that at a certain point in his life he was possessed by alcohol. If he was going to be free, he had to change his life. Some of his friends became "born-again" Christians but, sadly, these abrupt changes did not last. They tried to be people they were not. In the *mystagogia* period after his Baptism, Steve was trying to integrate his true self with his new life in Christ. He knew that being addicted got in the way of who he wanted to be: a husband, a father, a son of God. He knew he could not compromise. He would belong to God and to nothing else. St. Francois similarly speaks of his own complete commitment.

My heart is all God's own, longs only for the glory of his divine Majesty. We belong to him utterly, we have no am-bition except that of being called his own. If there were a single fibre of my heart not his or not cleaving to him I would tear it out at once; or some corner of my heart not marked by the crucifix, I would have none of it, no, not even for a moment.[17]

St. Francois also distrusted emotion as a foundation for long-term spiritual change. Emotions pass. Spiritual highs are in the end like any high: they can become addictive. St. Francois therefore said he wanted to live at the "topmost point of the spirit," high above passing emotion. If he prayed and felt nothing afterward, it said nothing about the quality of his prayer. If exterior events threatened to bring him down, he strove for detachment. "Accept your losses," he counseled. "Ask nothing, desire nothing, refuse nothing."[18] "Where there is less of our own choice there is more of God" was the test.[19]

"Accepting your losses" brings to my mind Millie. I met her at the time of the death of her husband, when she had to give up their home and move into a senior citizen apartment. "My life is becoming smaller," she said. But in fact it was becoming larger. She had always subsumed her life to others. She never considered herself worthy or competent. She recalled her father labeling her a dummy as a child. In her late sixties, with her new freedom, she began to pursue a college degree that she never thought herself capable of. She met new friends, younger ones with whom she was attending the university. They invited her to their social gatherings. She was discovering art and music and a talent for philosophy.

After three years of study Millie was diagnosed with cancer. Her dream of graduating now seemed impossible. The university, however, exempted her from her final requirements and in a special convocation for her alone she was awarded her degree. I was honored to give the invocation. Millie was free of her possessions, all of them. Her spirit was now able to follow its true course at last. By accepting her losses she gained infinitely more.

4. Belong Joyfully to God in the Midst of All You Do

The genius of St. Francois de Sales was to grasp that each of us has a personal calling from God that is our mission in life. We actually have three vocations. The one we all share is our vocation to holiness, given to us when we are baptized. Our baptismal calling can be lived out in various ways, as a priest, religious, married person, or single person: that is our second vocation. Within this second calling is another — the unique way we carry out the other two. Our particular gifts, the concrete circumstances of our life: these determine how we are to belong to God.

Sometimes we imagine what it would be like if our lives were totally different. We think of how holy we could be if only we had the opportunity to explore other options. We tend to trivialize our present life as something expendable, or not worthy. St. Francois had an answer for this sort of thinking. In writing to a married woman who was not always happy with her state in life, he said:

> Persevere in overcoming yourself in the little everyday frustrations that bother you; let your best efforts be directed there. God wishes nothing else of you at present, so don't waste time doing anything else. Don't sow your desires in someone else's garden, just cultivate your own as best you can; don't long to be other than what you are, but desire to be thoroughly what you are. Direct your thoughts to being very good at that and to bearing the crosses, little or great, that you will find there. Believe me, this is the most important and the least understood point in the spiritual life. We all love what is according to our taste; few people like what is according to their duty or to God's liking.

> What is the use of building castles in Spain when we have to live in France? This is my old lesson, and you grasp it well; but tell me, my dear, whether you are putting it into practice.

> I beg you to moderate your spiritual exercises, and in this regard give a good deal of weight to how your husband feels about them. Just laugh at these silly temptations in which the enemy depicts the world as a place to which you are obliged to return; laugh at these temptations, I say, as at something ridiculous. The only response to give them is that of our Lord, "Get behind me, Satan, you shall not tempt the Lord your God." My dear daughter, we are walking in the footsteps of the saints; let us go on courageously in spite of the difficulty we find there.[20]

To another married woman who claimed that her family duties did not allow much time to think about God, much less to spend hours in meditation and formal prayer, St. Francois gave this sage advice:

> We must love what God loves. He loves our vocation so let us also love it and not waste time thinking about other people's. Let us do our duty. Each person's cross is not too much for him or her. Be both Martha and Mary. Diligently carry out your duties, and often recollect yourself and put yourself in spirit at the feet of our Lord. Say, "My Lord, whether I'm rushing around or staying still, I am all yours and you are all mine. You are my first Spouse, and what I do is for love of you."[21]

In the biblical story, Martha and Mary and their brother, Lazarus, were hosting Jesus in their home in Bethany. Jesus and his male disciples discussed religious matters in the living room. Mary joined them there, while Martha stayed in the kitchen doing domestic chores. Martha interrupted the discussion and asked Jesus to tell Mary to return and join her in the kitchen, where she belonged. But Jesus welcomed the presence of Mary, even though the study of the Torah was forbidden to women by Jewish law. He replied, "Martha, Martha, you worry and fret about so many things, and yet few are needed, indeed only one. It is Mary who has chosen the better part, and it is not to be taken from her" (Luke 10:42–43). This story of Martha and Mary has often been used to contrast a higher, contemplative way of life practiced in the monastery or convent with a lower, active way of life lived out in the world. By interpreting the biblical story as saying we are called to be both Martha and Mary at the same time, St. Francois is saying that it is possible both to be engaged in the world and to have a rich spiritual life.

It has now become cliché to describe the spiritual life as a journey. The "journey" concept implies leaving our homes and embarking upon a wandering life. But Jesus can also be followed when we welcome him into our homes and ordinary life, just as Martha and Mary did. Joseph Power, commenting on another Bible story — of Jesus inviting himself into the home of Zaccheus — notes that this domestic spirituality is typically Salesian.

> In many ways Salesian spirituality is one of Jesus coming to
> our homes — to where we live, work, play, and pray. It is
> built on the dwelling of Jesus at home in our hearts through
> the gift of the Holy Spirit and thus enables us to "find" him
> where we are, in what we do, and in the relationships that
> form our lives. At the base of it all is the desire to "see" Jesus,
> and willingness to risk doing something creative about that
> desire.[22]

"Busyness," as it turns out, is not a distraction from the life of holiness; it can be holiness itself.

5. Do Each Day's Ordinary Things with Great Love

"Great works," St. Francois wrote, "lie not always in our way, but every moment we may do little ones with excellence, that is, with great love."[23] Love is the measure, not the deed. Even a cup of water given to one of Christ's least ones does not go without its reward. We should recall that the salvation of the world by Christ was not accomplished by heroic deeds but in kitchens and on streets and in markets and places of worship, in one-on-one encounters and conversations.

For this reason St. Francois stresses practicing those virtues that are appropriate to our particular state in life. He writes, "Occasions do not often present themselves for the exercise of fortitude,

magnanimity, and great generosity, but meekness, temperance, integrity, and humility are virtues that must mark all our actions in
life.... In practicing the virtues we should prefer the one most
conformable to our duties rather than one more agreeable to our
tastes. Each person must practice in a special manner the virtues
needed by the kind of life he is called to."[24]

Meekness, mildness, and modesty are highly honored in the
spirituality of St. Francois even if they do not count for much
in the self-promoting aggressive culture we are accustomed to.
St. Francois calls these the "little virtues," but they are not little
in terms of making life pleasant and easy for everyone. And if
you have ever tried to live them, they are certainly not easy in
practice.

> *If it is not something you can do
> every day, it is not real.*

One of the key concepts of Salesian spirituality differentiates
what is called the "love of conformity" and the "love of submission." We are called upon to love God by conforming to his will
as he has made it known in all his commandments and counsels.
This is the love of conformity. We also love God by submitting
ourselves to all the circumstances of our life as these are given to
us every day. If we love God in both these ways we need not be
concerned that holiness is eluding us. How good do we have to
be? Just this much is enough.

These five spiritual principles encapsulate a way of living that
is best expressed in its adverbs: listen deeply, commit firmly, strive
gently, belong joyfully, do daily. They express a spirituality that
seeks inner transformation rather than exterior display. It stresses

the need for firm, rigorous practice. It is opposed to sudden, vio-
lent change and prefers small steps. If it is not joyful, it is not of
God. And if it is not something you can do every day, it is not
real. Ends, even great spiritual ends, do not justify means. Means
are everything. The path itself is the destination. Heaven is the
way to heaven, for Jesus is the way. Live Jesus.

Two

Seeking a Spiritual Guide

Steve had no spiritual mentor to guide him in the critical early phases of his life. His stepfather resorted to physical punishment — his belt — to enforce discipline. When Steve had to take over his stepfather's business, he did not have anyone to guide him. These experiences made him even more resolved to be a good father to his children.

St. Francois did not have a good relationship with his father either. Like Steve, he felt a lot of anger, which he knew he needed to control. The advice St. Francois was given seemed not to coincide with his lived experience. Both Steve and St. Francois had to fall back upon what their hearts told them was right. Ultimately, this is true for everyone.

Each of us belongs to God; only God can plumb the depths and riches of our hearts, which are made for him alone. Finding a compatible soul who can serve as our spiritual guide in our search for God is an especially difficult undertaking.

The Need for a Spiritual Guide

Early in his *Introduction* St. Francois speaks of the "need of a guide for beginning devotion and making progress in it."[1] He cites the example of St. Teresa of Avila, a Spanish mystic and religious reformer (1515–82). In her enthusiasm, St. Teresa needed the moderating influence of someone more experienced than she in spiritual matters. Here and in all his writings St. Francois describes the posture of the person seeking direction as one of "obedience" to the guide or director. This may strike us as uncongenial, given our more skeptical approach even to experts, but religious obedience has a special and unique quality that makes this virtue a *sine qua non* for successful spiritual direction. Obedience comes from a Latin word that means "to hear" or "to listen." Far from connoting a servile subjection to the whims and fancies of another, obedience implies a deep and respectful mutual listening on the parts of director and directee. The director must be committed to attending with sensitivity and alertness to the movements of the soul of the one coming for direction, and the directee must commit complete trust and willingness to follow the advice or counsel of the director. For scrupulous souls, promising "obedience" to the advice being given is often the liberation they need from their own constant second-guessing.

St. Francois says we need guidance from another to make a good start in the spiritual life, to lay solid foundations upon which to build. Knowing when to challenge and when to comfort and console are skills developed by the good director. The director will know, too, how to stress the values that underlie religious practices and can detect when overemphasis upon the practices can undermine the values being sought. For example, St. Vincent de Paul, a friend of St. Francois de Sales, once counseled that we should not be disturbed if our prayers are interrupted by someone in need. We should remember that helping others is itself a form of prayer.

The person being directed is also invited to use complete candor and honesty. Because the advice of the director is to be considered God's own voice addressing us, it would be foolish to hide anything from God because God knows everything from the start. In this sense, the director has to have a supreme objectivity in interpreting God's will for the person under his or her care, never compromising the higher Gospel standards to which we are called even in our human weakness.

The Qualities of a Good Spiritual Guide

Objectivity and the capacity for deep empathetic listening are essential qualities to be sought in any spiritual director. St. Francois also says that a good spiritual director should be a person of charity, knowledge, and prudence.[2] He describes the ideal director as one with whom we have a high degree of personal comfort. We are supposed to be able easily to turn to our director for support, encouragement, and reassurance when we need it. For this reason the spiritual director is always the one to be sought out by the person seeking direction and never the other way around.

Other qualities that we seek in our spiritual director are the abilities to heal our hearts, to give firm guidance, to protect us from harm, and to be, above all, a good friend. St. Francois concludes, "For this purpose choose one out of a thousand, as Avila says. For my part, I say one out of ten thousand, for there are fewer men than we realize who are capable of this task."[3]

What Is Spiritual Direction?

Perhaps the best place to start in defining the nature of the interaction we call "spiritual direction" is to distinguish it from two other types of interpersonal encounter that are closely related to it — counseling or therapy, and sacramental confession.

A counselor or therapist is a professional person trained to assist in times of emotional distress and life crises. The professional may employ skills of psychological analysis and medication to provide insight and bring about relief. People who are not functioning well in terms of thinking processes or personal relations and other life skills may not be capable of benefiting from spiritual direction until their life is in order. People suffering from addictions will need to find remedies for their dependency apart from spiritual direction, although in all these cases spiritual direction may be of immense help and support.

Psychotherapy, of course, did not exist at the time of St. François, and so no doubt some of the symptoms he treated in spiritual direction might be more accurately identified today as of the psychological rather than the spiritual realm. The spiritual and the psychological issues were treated together.

St. François also tended to merge sacramental confession with spiritual direction. Nowadays the confessor is often a priest who is not necessarily the one to whom one goes regularly for spiritual direction. The circumstances of the administration of the Sacrament of Reconciliation often do not permit the kind of extended exchange that spiritual direction requires.

Spiritual direction has as its purpose assisting a person to listen to the voice of the Holy Spirit speaking in his or her heart. The goal of spiritual direction is the achievement of perfect freedom in listening to and following the Spirit's lead. The director will be of help in assisting the person to distinguish the voice of the Holy Spirit from the voice of the other spirit, the spirit of evil. Medieval art often depicts a person with two spirits speaking into separate ears, the one being the Paraclete, or Advocate, who pleads our cause and takes our side, the other the Satan, the accuser, the detractor, the source of temptation. According to St. Paul and St. Ignatius of Loyola after him, we can distinguish the source of the words we are hearing within us by their effects on our own spirit. The "fruits" of the Holy Spirit are "love, joy, peace, patience, kindness, goodness, trustfulness, gentleness, and self-control" (Gal. 5:22). The effects of the evil spirit are equally transparent and detectable: self-preoccupation, anxiety, division, jealousy, sensuality, envy, and angry disposition (Gal. 5:19–20). What is of God will show itself by the positive effects it has upon our spirits; what is not of God will manifest the reverse.

Prayer experiences are often the subject matter presented in spiritual direction. The spiritual effects of prayer, the insights and resolutions that emerge from it, are shared and confirmed. Since prayer or meditation, according to St. Francois, is the principal means of our ongoing conversion to the Gospel, fidelity to prayer is a constant theme of spiritual direction.

According to St. Francois, the means a good spiritual director uses in direction is friendship. Sometimes it is said, accurately, that a spiritual director is a "soul friend." Citing words of Scripture, St. Francois describes the director as "a faithful friend": "A faithful friend is a strong defense, and he who has found one has found a treasure" (Sir. 6:14). He also calls spiritual direction "befriending." Such a friend is a source of "wisdom in affliction, sorrow, and failure."[4] This friend will provide support or correction depending upon our needs.

Spiritual Direction Today

While it has always been difficult to find a suitable person for spiritual direction, the task is even more difficult today. A spiritual director need not be a priest, although St. Francois assumed so, but finding a competent, trained person to serve as a spiritual guide has never been harder. And so in our spiritual need, we often rely upon spiritual reading for inspiration and guidance. Books of spirituality are proliferating, and for good reason.

Probably most spiritual direction today is being given by the few close friends with whom we maintain ongoing regular contact. It is not unnatural to look to our everyday friends for spiritual help even if we do not often identify it as such. Our friends have the luxury of being honest with us because we know their love is genuine. The cultivation of friends, therefore, is an essential spiritual task for everyone. Spiritual conversion is sometimes described as coming to accept the opinion of one's friends. But this type of counsel is better termed "spiritual companionship" rather than spiritual direction as such.

"How is your heart? And is your heart in your hands?"

Still there remains the value of having a director who is trained for the task, and is a holy person himself or herself. This value is increased if the director is a priest to whom we can go for sacramental confession as an essential part of the process of spiritual direction.

While having your own spiritual director, like having your own trainer to keep physically fit, may be ideal, the day-in, day-out spiritual direction that the Church provides to everyone is the lectionary of biblical readings. Daily meditation upon the texts of the lectionary of Mass readings for each day and taking them to heart is a route to conversion that is open to all. Group spiritual direction is becoming more common and may be a good first step.

The real spiritual director, of course, is the Holy Spirit. The wise human guide strives to attend to what the Holy Spirit is saying to the individual soul. St. Francois understood this very well. For nineteen years, Ste. Jeanne-Francoise de Chantal benefited from St. Francois's spiritual direction. This is how she describes her experience of his direction:

Cooperating with the Holy Spirit who guided him, he swiftly but unhurriedly formed a true picture of the soul before him, and if he judged the person unready for what he wanted to say, he would keep his counsel, not wanting to waste words where there was no real audience. But the moment he recognized the Holy Spirit at work in a soul, he lavished on it all the teaching and instruction needed for its personal way of salvation. I also noticed that he preferred to leave souls quite free so that the Spirit could lead them while he himself followed on behind, letting souls act on divine inspiration rather than on his own personal instructions. I know that this is how he directed me and I have heard the same from others who were well qualified to appreciate his methods; and if I have understood this rightly it proves that his insight into souls was most enlightened and that he had the faculty of distinguishing spiritual influences in others.[5]

A Spiritual Direction Session with St. Francois

In his posture of being a good listener, St. Francois asked two questions of a spiritual directee — questions that seem very simple but actually require much introspection. His first was, "How is your heart?" His second, "Is your heart in your hands?"

"How is your heart?" may be something we have never been asked before, not even by ourselves. We are acculturated to attend to the exterior agenda, the expectations of others and the burdens we have placed upon ourselves, and rarely, if ever, ask ourselves where our heart is in all this and what are the personal costs for maintaining our present existence. We are shaped by our culture to delay and sacrifice our pleasure and happiness to dangerous lengths. We do not notice the price we are paying in terms of wear and tear on our spirits from our workaholism and failure to attend to our spiritual and physical needs for refreshment and renewal. We feel caught in an iron cage of obligations, and to want to escape them may strike us as selfish and indulgent.

Our conversion to Christ must start with our hearts and then move outward to our actions and attitudes. St. Francois wisely observes, "Since the heart is the source of our actions, as the heart is so are they."[6] He asks us as part of our response to the first question to recall what delights us and nourishes us and to remember the happiest times in our lives, the times when we were most ourselves. Do we recognize ourselves anymore? If our spirituality does not begin with an awareness of our heart and its needs but rather covers over the heart with a rigid set of additional burdens and duties, our heart will work a terrible vengeance. St. Irenaeus, a second-century Father of the Church, memorably wrote that "the glory of God is the human person fully alive."[7]

Jesus once observed that a house swept clean of demons but left empty will soon fill up with other demons that are far worse (Matt. 12:43–45). We must learn what can truly fill our hearts with delight and satisfy our deepest desires or we may find ourselves on a self-destructive path. Jesus declared, "I have come that they may have life, life in all its fullness" (John 10:10).

St. Francois's second question — "Are you holding your heart in your hands?"[8] — asks us whether we have a sufficient love of our own hearts and think of our hearts enough. Is our heart in disarray and disordered, torn by various passions — "love, hatred, desire, hope, sadness and joy"?[9] Are we experiencing our life as out of control? Are our priorities correct? Are we just going through the motions or are our hearts truly in what we do? It will take much work and patience to heal our "entangled heart."[10]

How to Handle Anger (with Care!): A Case Study of Salesian Spirituality

Let's look at the handling of the common emotion of anger to explore the riches of Salesian spirituality. It is a good example to take because St. Francois speaks not only of his experience of other people's problems but also of his own. St. Francois's temperament was passionate and volatile. It was only by much hard spiritual work that he gained the reputation of being entirely the opposite — a person of gentle disposition conveying the presence of God to whomever he met.

In the *Testimony*, which Ste. Jeanne-Francoise composed as part of the process of the canonization of St. Francois, she mentions the impression he made upon Pierre Cardinal Bérulle as an example of the common estimation people had of him.

> Monsieur de Bérulle, a man of great and rare virtue, piety, and learning, superior of the Oratorians in France, once said to a nun who mentioned it to me, that his peace was *imperturbable*. He had this treasure in himself and was also able to pass it on to everyone who came anywhere near him; and one just can't say how many people there were who went to him all anxious and upset, and came away soothed and at peace. I speak of what I know personally; this has been my own very frequent experience and that of many others whom I know. It was commonly said that he had the gift of imparting peace of soul to those who came to talk to him.[11]

In 1614, in one of his thousands of letters of spiritual direction, St. Francois addressed the problem of anger, which a certain Madame de la Fléchère had presented to him. He admits to speaking out of personal experience when imparting his counsel to her.

"Take reassurance for your spirit," he writes, "for this is not something I haven't experienced myself. I know well that our nature boils with bitterness when we feel ourselves under attack and we let our self-esteem suggest all kinds of bad feelings against those who are doing the attack. With God's help we can try to resist being enraged or at least to give in completely. This then is a good opportunity to practice humility, to confound our enemy with sweetness, and to acknowledge our miserableness."[12]

This letter is a perfect summary of the more extensive treatment of how to handle anger that St. Francois gives in the *Introduction to the Devout Life*. His advice can be summed up thus:

1. Anger is a normal human reaction when we feel we are being attacked or hurt.

2. We cannot control other people's behavior toward us but we can control our own reactions.

3. Recognize that it's our vanity, our self-centeredness, our pride (*amour-propre*) more than anything else that's involved.

4. Say a prayer and ask for God's help.

5. Try not to let the behavior of others make you lose control completely but if you fail, at least moderate your response.

6. Use the occasion to practice the virtue of humility and thereby turn a negative into a positive experience.

7. Confound your enemy by not retaliating in kind but reacting with sweetness, recalling what Scripture teaches, that by such kindness you are placing hot coals on your enemy's head (Rom. 12:20).

8. Allow your propensity for anger to help you recognize your own limitations.

The *Introduction* elaborates upon these pithy words of advice. It is not humility that is urged as the positive virtue to be practiced to counter our angry impulses, but meekness. St. Francois's favorite passage in all of Scripture was the words of Jesus quoted earlier about learning from his meek and humble heart, thus relieving ourselves of many heavy self-imposed burdens (Matt. 11:28–30). These two virtues, humility and meekness, are called by St. Francois the "favorite and beloved" of the Lord himself. "Humility perfects us with respect to God, and meekness with respect to our neighbor."[13]

---

*Accept the temperament you were
born with and go with it.*

The cultivation of meekness helps because, besides being numbered by Jesus among the very blessings given to those who follow his Gospel, meekness directly addresses the issue of violence in our hearts. Sometimes in their effort to overcome anger people become angry with themselves for being angry. "So too it often happens that by trying violently to restrain our anger, we stir up more trouble within our heart than wrath existed before and being thus agitated our heart can no longer be its own master."[14] In other words, we should practice meekness and gentleness not only with regard to others but toward our own spirit, accepting our own imperfections.

St. Francois instructs, "We must not fret over our own imperfections."[15] In fact, he tells us we should even love them.[16] The word he uses for limitations, imperfections, or what we might call creatureliness, is "abjections." In French this word signifies miserableness or wretchedness. As humble people we should be willing not only to admit our abject state but to love it and delight in it, he counsels. It's part of the acquisition of the religious wisdom that we are not God.

> There are even faults that involve no other ill except abjection. Humility does not require that we should deliberately commit such faults but it does require that we should not disturb ourselves when we have committed them.[17]

Rather than be down on ourselves if we have done or said anything out of anger that was an offense against a neighbor, we should simply repent and be sorry and make the best amends we can.[18] Don't even try to redesign yourself but accept the temperament you were born with and go with it. For someone like St. Francois, who was subject to excessive scrupulousness, this must have come as hard-won wisdom.

Sometimes anger is justified, but in this regard he cites with approval the advice of St. Augustine: "It is better to deny entrance to just and reasonable anger than to admit it, no matter how small it is. Once let in, it is driven out again only with difficulty."[19] In sum, St. Francis states, "It is better to attempt to find a way to live without anger than to pretend to make a moderate, discreet use of it."[20]

Wendy Wright, a Salesian scholar, describes how astonishing it was to be taught through her study of St. Francois that she could be comfortable with and even claim those parts of herself that she might not previously have wished to acknowledge. She writes:

> Gradually I began to find a referent, something I knew to be deeply life-giving in my own spiritual journey, against which to evaluate the teaching on "love your abjections." I began to live into my own limitations, those pesky arenas of brokenness and blindness that seem always to be there whether

we want them or not. Gradually I began (as mid-life neared) to realize that my task was not so much to eliminate them, for this was in fact impossible, although I could certainly work on them. Rather my task was to recognize and accept them. My abjections were my unwanted limitations. It was then that the radical wisdom of the *Introduction* became clear to me. For its call was not simply to accept, but to *love*, my abjections. What could this mean? To embrace, to cherish those parts of the self that one would prefer not to claim, much less to make public. What an astonishing thought. But the more I lived with this and the more I let it unfold as an experience of self-revelation in prayer, the more I began to delight in it. To *love* our abjections is to love ourselves in our wholeness, *as we are loved* by God, and thus it is to enter into God's infinite compassion. To love our abjections is indeed a sublime spiritual teaching.[21]

"The Particular Examen" as a Way to Handle Anger

When I was in seminary we followed a community rule based loosely upon the Spiritual Exercises of St. Ignatius of Loyola. These same Exercises guided St. Francois during his student days at the College of Clérmont in Paris. In addition to daily meditation at 6:00 a.m. and the general examination of conscience at night, we were led through what was called "the particular examen" just before lunch. During that fifteen-minute period, we were to select a particular virtue or vice to concentrate upon. It was only years later when I returned to the seminary as its rector that I learned that this was not at all the particular examen that St. Ignatius had in mind. Studies conducted in the late twentieth century found that the particular examen of St. Ignatius was not about any particular virtue or vice but exclusively about what you have come to know as your own deepest vice and its virtuous opposite. Every day we are to return, in time set aside for the particular examen, to our greatest imperfection and then flip it over into its opposite, making the positive virtue our mantra.

In his practice of the particular examen, St. Francois, knowing his vice was a volatile temperament, worked every day of his life on the virtue of *douceur,* sweetness. Ste. Jeanne-Francoise describes what he tried to do.

> Our saint was not spared from actually feeling emotions and passions, he did not approve of people wanting to be free of them; but the only notice he took of them was to rein them in hard, and he said he found real joy in doing this. He also said that passions helped to call out and exercise the most worthwhile virtues and establish passions with such absolute authority that they obeyed him like slaves, and toward the end of his life there was hardly any outward sign of them.[22]

Steve found a way to channel his anger into something good. He used his frustrations to give him an edge in sports: getting angry at the competing team is a way of letting go of frustration. Steve turned anger into competitiveness, just as St. Francois funneled his passionate nature into zeal.

Finding a Spiritual Director

It might be helpful to offer some advice on how to find a spiritual director for yourself. Since spiritual directors are often reluctant to advertise and may not charge for their services, they commonly become known by word of mouth.

Going on a retreat at a spiritual center is a good way to become acquainted with their staffs and to learn about their resources. Some dioceses provide lists of approved spiritual directors. The local parish priests may also have much useful information.

In the end, the selection of a spiritual director is a highly personal decision. Success is not guaranteed the first time around.

Three

Developing a Personal Rule of Life

Much like people today checking out the self-help or spirituality section of a bookstore, the first Christians looked to Jesus as a teacher of wisdom and as a guide for daily living. "Wisdom" in the way that word was used at that time refers to the practical knowledge needed to manage the concrete details of living; it was not theoretical at all. One wisdom saying of Jesus that comes to mind as we approach the topic of a personal rule of life for ourselves is this:

> So long as a strong man fully armed guards his own palace, his goods are undisturbed; but when someone stronger than he is attacks and defeats him, the stronger man takes away all the weapons he relied on and shares out his spoil.
>
> (Luke 11:21–22)

This sounds obvious but this word of wisdom is often overlooked. Jesus himself was that strong man who never let anything that happened to him upset his rock-solid relationship with the One he called Father. Jesus is referred to as the rock of our salvation. We too, if we are to be successful, must put into place solid foundations that will carry us through any difficulty.

In another wisdom saying Jesus speaks about the necessity of building our house upon a solid foundation dug deep in the ground. He contrasts this house with one built upon sand:

> When the river was in flood it bore down on that house but could not shake it, it was so well built. But the one who listens and does nothing is like the man who built his house on sand, with no foundations: as soon as the river bore down on it, it collapsed; and what a ruin that house became!
>
> (Luke 6:48–49)

In other words, in life, we have to make accurate calculations about what will be needed for the long haul.

One of Jesus' parables tells the story of a devious employee who, without authorization, offers discounts to customers who might be able to offer him a job should he become unemployed. The parable seems to look favorably upon dishonesty. In fact, it is calling attention to the employee's astute behavior in making provision for his future. Even children of the light, Jesus concludes, need a similar astuteness (Luke 16:8).

America is known as the birthplace of pragmatism, a philosophy that espouses "Does it work?" as the criterion of truth. It may seem amazing to us that Jesus himself favors a results-based philosophy of life: by their fruits you shall know them, he says. "There is no sound tree that produces rotten fruit, nor again a rotten tree that produces sound fruit. Every tree can be told by its own fruit" (Luke 6:43–44).

Developing a personal rule of life based upon Gospel principles for living is a helpful means of creating solid structures and routines to fall back upon. Those who create such a rule of life should have an accurate idea of what they personally need for a happy and productive life.

Creating Our Own Inner *Cortile*

Italian architecture has long been based upon the strict separation of public and private zones of living. The inner, private living spaces were completely guarded from the vicissitudes of weather, business, and outside events by an exterior that gave no indication as to what was inside. Exterior facades of the most elaborate palaces were austere and plain and looked like fortresses.

At the center of the inner, private space was the rectangular *cortile*, or courtyard, onto which the windows and the doors of the house opened. The *cortile* itself most often had a gushing fountain that gave the illusion even in the hottest weather of refreshing coolness and watery abundance. Lush trees, flowers, and plantings created an oasis of calm and peace in the midst of a bustling, noisy, densely settled urban environment.

The *cortile* of Roman architecture illustrates the function of a personal rule of life: it is the exterior structure designed to protect an inviolable inner space.

The *cortile* was a good image for Steve to latch onto since he finds great peace in building things. One long-term project for his free time is constructing a log cabin on an island off the coast of Maine. The fireplace, made of local stone, is a source of particular pride. On the mainland and back at his usual routine he can visualize the house on the island to give him the perspective he needs not to get lost in the details of daily obligations.

Maybe for Steve those stretches of time spent concentrating on making natural materials into something that will stand for a long time is a form of meditation. In fact, I am sure it is. Gym time is also time alone that brings Steve spiritual as well as physical benefits. Noontime basketball games with friends are a good means to work off frustrations. Regular laps in the pool also have a calming effect.

The danger for Steve is letting the time he spends lying on his recliner with the television remote in his hand become a substitute for spiritual and intellectual growth. Lethargy, which in the technical language of spirituality is called "acedia," can be devastating if indulged in too long. Finding the right rhythm is a challenge for Steve — and for anyone else.

Elements of a Personal Rule of Life

St. Augustine in the *Confessions* outlined the four elements of a truly fulfilling and satisfying life that no doubt inspired St. Francois and many others. They are: meditation, which is the source of deepest pleasure; physical exercise; intellectual development; and service to others by means of our work.[1] In the second part of the *Introduction*, St. Francois draws out a daily program for the meditation element of a full and balanced life.

1. Immediately upon arising, do your morning prayer exercises which will prepare you mentally and spiritually for the day. Adore God and thank God for the gift of a new day. Make a firm resolution to use the day only for God. Ask God's help in handling the day's duties, anticipating anything that may be particularly stressful so that you may be spiritually ready to face it.

2. Do your regular hour of meditation without fail. If you cannot fit it in at the start of the day, try to meditate before lunchtime.

3. Attend daily Mass, if possible.

4. Offer brief prayers in the course of the day as a kind of spiritual retreat you can fall back on in the midst of other activities.

5. Find time for some spiritual reading, however brief: the Bible, lives of saints, and other works of inspiration.

6. At the end of the day, examine your conscience about how the day has gone and ask God's forgiveness for failings.

7. Before falling asleep commend to the Lord's care all your loved ones and the needs of the world as well as your own.

St. Francois also advises that we may be helped in our daily living by being part of a group of like-minded friends ("confraternities," as he calls them), who may share our values and routines of prayer with us. Joining in the Church's Liturgy of the Hours would be a good example of a supportive and helpful group religious activity. He also counsels weekly sacramental confession of sins as an aid to devotion and an encouragement in our spiritual strivings even if we are not aware of any serious transgressions.[2]

These elements of daily prayer constitute the nucleus of the Spiritual Directory St. Francois and Ste. Jeanne-Francoise developed as the rule of life for their Visitandine nuns. St. Francois sets them forth in the *Introduction* as helpful for laypeople as well as for nuns in convents. In this way, St. Francois demonstrates that holiness of life is a possibility for all, even those who do not have the luxury of spending their days in monastic enclosures but have to fulfill demanding worldly obligations.

Necessary Adaptations

St. Francois would be the first to say that even these modest and measured spiritual practices may have to be modified and adapted according to the particular circumstances we find ourselves in. For St. Francois, the preservation of the basic values was always to be emphasized over the specific practices designed to put them into action. Wendy Wright summarizes well the essence of this spiritual approach. Speaking of the Visitandines, she says:

> The interior practice of the presence of God took the place of long prayers, detachment from things supplanted absolute poverty, mortification of spirit replaced bodily penance, charity modified radical solitude, and obedience to small observances stood in place of obvious austerity. Theirs was to be a hidden life of perfection acquired through the practice of the little virtues of humility, simplicity, gentleness, charity and resignation.[3]

When he was first made bishop, the office and its responsibilities caused a certain disruption in St. Francois's prayer routines. Later on he was able to handle things better as he indicates in a letter to Ste. Jeanne-Francoise written in September 1607:

> You give me great pleasure in one of your letters to ask me if I am praying. O my daughter, do so, always ask about the state of my soul because I know well that your curiosity in this area comes from the ardor of the charity you have for me. Yes, my daughter, through the grace of God I am able to maintain more mental prayer than before, for there is not a single day that passes without it, except for the occasional Sunday when I have to hear confessions. And if on those occasions when God gives me the strength to get up before the day begins for this purpose, I anticipate the multitude of the day's embarrassments and do so jauntily. I would like to be able to do such prayer twice a day, but that's impossible.[4]

I like the word St. Francois uses for the things that happen to us during a typical day: "embarrassments," the daily embarrassments. I'm sure a sensitive soul like his was embarrassed and put upon many times in the rough round of pastoral duties. He claims that by meditating he can keep his composure in this potentially unsettling milieu. Besides the hour of meditation each day, he would celebrate Mass and pray the Rosary. Hearing confessions was always part of his pastoral practice and he did so on demand. He usually did office work in the morning and in the afternoon was available for any member of his flock to see him about their issues and problems. In between he would make home visits to the sick and poor in Annecy and find time to write twenty to thirty letters to those seeking his spiritual advice.[5]

Holiness of life is a possibility for all, even those who do not have the luxury of spending their days in monastic enclosures.

A lot of his time in these years of episcopal service went into the preparation of his homilies. In this labor he had to do some study and much prayer; thus he could combine private devotion with public activity. Ste. Jeanne-Francoise speaks of this habit of his, which represented a major adjustment in his prayer routines to meet his pastoral schedule of duties.

He turned every incident to good account spiritually, drawing good thoughts from everything that happened to him. The great moment for these spiritual lights was when he was preparing his sermons, and this he usually did while pacing up and down in his room or when out walking. He told me that his prayer was nourished by his study, and that after reading he felt greatly enlightened and full of fervour.[6]

St. Francois always had the tendency to overwork. The strains that came from this had harmful effects on his body and soul. As the years went on he suffered from overweight and a variety of illnesses, and had less time for prayer. Ste. Jeanne-Francoise explains:

For several years before he died he was hardly able to set aside any time for prayer, because he was overwhelmed by work; and one day when I asked him whether he had prayed, he said, "No, but it comes to the same thing." For he never lost his union with God, and he used to say that in this life we must pray by our work and action. His own life was certainly an uninterrupted prayer.[7]

The temptation to make your work your prayer is not a good one, especially if no time is set aside from work specifically for prayer. The fact that St. Francois succumbed to this temptation and felt he had no choice in the matter should be encouraging to us who also find our lives constantly falling out of balance, and the element being sacrificed is always prayer. We can take some comfort by realizing that the Kingdom of God does not yet rule the earth. Jesus asks us to pray "Thy kingdom come" because we know the world and its structures are not governed by spiritual priorities. We always have to fight to find space for God and for our own mental and spiritual health. Even great saints did not always succeed in that fight. What made them saints was that even while failing they continued to believe in the necessity of prayer and the priority of God in their lives and never gave up the effort to honor these in practice. Success does not mean doing everything perfectly well, but rather never ceasing to try. As Mother Teresa of Calcutta often said, "God does not ask us to be successful but to be faithful."

The Rule of Life of
Terence Cardinal Cooke

During my years as rector of the North American College in Rome I developed a friendship with the archbishop of New York, Terence Cardinal Cooke (1921–82). During his frequent visits to the Vatican on official business, he always stayed with us at the seminary. In the surroundings of Rome, away from the pressures of the archdiocese, Cardinal Cooke could relax and talk with us over meals and in the faculty lounge. In those conversations I learned the humility of the man and the extraordinary kindness that was his hallmark virtue. He consciously and deliberately, I believe, refrained from saying anything bad about anyone.

Very frequently I would turn to Cardinal Cooke for support and advice. Even when he was not a member of the seminary's board of bishops, he would generously attend a late meeting of the board during the semiannual bishops' conferences at my invitation and assist my efforts with the bishops in any way he could. It was only after his death that we learned that during all the years that I knew him, he was being treated for lymphoma. These treatments were never allowed to impede the demanding schedule of his involvements and service.

When Cardinal Cooke was thirty-one years old and had been ordained for seven years, he composed for himself a rule of life that he adhered to through all the years of his priesthood and episcopate until his death. Over time he amended it, making it stricter, not looser, and signing his name once again. The seminary that trains priests has a structured life of prayer, study, and service; to ensure that, in the chaotic demands of actual pastoral ministry, the priest transfers some structures into his personal life. Many, like Cardinal Cooke, draw up a personal Rule after ordination. Here is the Rule that Cardinal Cooke adopted for himself.

Surrender to the Will of God

Jesus must be the life of my work. "I do not call you servants but friends."

1. Monthly day of recollection — Thursday before or after first Friday or Manhattan Day of recollection;

2. At least — a weekly Friday Holy Hour;

3. Weekly confessions — Friday or Saturday morning, try to get definite director;

4. Anticipate Divine Office — after breakfast, before or after supper;

5. Daily schedule:

    (a) rising one hour before Mass for prayer and meditation;

    (b) read Divine Office (as above);

    (c) Visits and Rosary — Chapel of Our Lady of Charity;

    (d) Prayers during the day — Angelus, Aspirations, Rosary — Have the mind of Christ, good example, bring others to Christ, work for His Glory, for souls;

    (e) Evening visit at the Cenacle;

    (f) Spiritual Reading — after breakfast, if possible and in the evening;

    (g) Evening — prayers, general examen, meditation points.[8]

This rule of life, this inner *cortile* of peaceful communion with God, was the solid rock foundation that preserved Cardinal Cooke from faltering under his heavy burden of duties and living with a fatal illness.

What is remarkable about this personal Rule composed in the twentieth century is that it is practically identical with the spiritual program laid out by St. Francois three hundred years earlier. How widely and how deeply has the Ignatian and Salesian spirituality pervaded modern Catholicism!

How to Design a Personal Rule of Life

We have looked at a rule of life developed by St. Francois and Ste. Jeanne-Francoise for nuns and the one Cardinal Cooke established for himself. However, nuns and clerics often have a more orderly existence than most laypeople enjoy. The key to designing your own rule of life is to start with what you have to do every day and try to do it all the best you can, for the glory of God and the salvation of your soul and that of others.

The great nineteenth-century churchman John Henry Cardinal Newman wrote a meditation on the theme "A Short Road to Perfection." It is not surprising that he would base his reflection on a basic principle of the spiritual life as taught by St. Francois de Sales, for he greatly admired St. Francois and kept a picture of him on the wall above the altar in his private chapel. Newman calls the way to perfection "short," not in the sense of a shortcut or an easy way to holiness, but short in the sense of pertinent to our actual way of living. This is what St. Francois meant when he said that our basic religious duty is to our particular state in life. Newman goes on to say that to be perfect means nothing heroic but merely trying to be consistent in all that we do. He sees the value of being very concrete in setting down our goals so that perfection doesn't become a vague notion that we just talk about. He concludes:

He, then, is perfect who does the work of the day perfectly, and we need not go beyond this to seek for perfection. You need not go out of the round of the day.[9]

To design your own rule of life, then, you must see how you can fit in the four values St. Augustine identified as characteristic of a fulfilling life: regular communion with God ("meditation"), physical exercise, mental growth, and service to others. Service to others most often takes the form of the actual job or profession we perform to make a living. Prayer and meditation should be regular but how and when it takes place each day must arise out of our particular circumstances. Our intellectual development can take various forms like personal reading, discussion groups, travel, continuing education courses, visits to museums, and many other things. Health clubs and personal trainers have proven to be of great help to those who can afford them in keeping themselves in good physical shape. Regular visits to the doctor and dentist might well be incorporated into a rule of life.

The key to designing your own rule of life is to start with what you have to do every day and try to do it all the best you can.

Cardinal Newman himself provides his own practical list of daily activities that make for a well-rounded life, or what he calls "perfection":

If you ask me what you are to do in order to be perfect, I say, first — Do not lie in bed beyond the due time of rising; give your first thoughts to God; make a good visit to the

Blessed Sacrament; say the Angelus devoutly; eat and drink to God's glory; say the Rosary well; be recollected; keep out bad thoughts; make your evening meditation well; examine yourself daily; go to bed in good time, and you are already perfect.[10]

Four

The Goal of the Spiritual Life: Falling in Love with God

St. Francois addresses his readers, beginners in the spiritual life, as "Philothee," which literally means "one who has fallen in love with God." In a similar way, St. Luke wrote both his Gospel and the Acts of the Apostles for "Theophilus," a Greek name that means the same thing. How is it possible for a human being to fall in love with God? Can we feel any equality with God, the creator of the heavens and the earth? When we encounter the reality of God, can our reaction be anything other than awe and wonder and a sense of our own sinfulness? Would not individuals claiming God as their ultimate Lover be deluding themselves or, perhaps in a dangerous way, substituting a supposed divine love for a human love they feel deprived of?

These questions are all valid. And yet no one who has not had some experience of being loved by God could ever be introduced to the spiritual life. As St. John tells us, reflecting at the end of his life on his experience of knowing Jesus, "Anyone who fails to love can never have known God, because God is love" (1 John 4:7). The spiritual life begins for us when we recognize that God's love for us is behind every experience we've had of love. Whenever and wherever we know genuine love, we are becoming acquainted with God.

When we fall in love we know what an incredible, undeserved gift we have received. The love bestowed on us by another can never be coerced or bought no matter how hard we try; love, if it is love, is freely given. When we have it we feel fantastically blessed, graced, and fortunate beyond all deserving. We feel a tremendous self-affirmation; we see ourselves forever after in a different way, as someone exceptional.

But often it happens that God's love is discovered when we have the opposite experience — of not being loved at all, of being lost, overwhelmed, and aware of our inadequacy, sinfulness, and failure. This happened to Steve at the age of nineteen. This was also the experience that led Ste. Marguerite Marie Alacoque (1647–90) to the revelation of the Sacred Heart of Jesus. Drawing upon their experiences, and those of others, we can understand more deeply what falling in love with God truly means.

An Experience of the Revelation of Divine Love: Aaron

Steve was introduced to God's love for him early in life when an angel told him that he would be all right. During the *mystagogia* period after his Baptism he returned to that experience and connected it with new signs of God's love — the holy sacraments he had just received.

Aaron was another man to whom I gave spiritual direction. Unlike Steve, Aaron had been a Catholic all his life but had never consciously been aware of God's love until adulthood. When I met him for the first time he was twenty-nine and had begun a career as a children's advocate and social worker.

In Aaron's home the Catholic faith was important. His mother was a teacher in a Catholic school and a lector at Mass. But when he went away to college Aaron enjoyed his new freedom, including the freedom not to attend Mass anymore. It was only after graduation that he began to feel something was missing. His life was going reasonably well, but it did not hang together. He was, in some way he could not describe, dissatisfied. One of his New Year's resolutions was to go back to church.

> *"I learned for the first time in my life that I could have a personal relationship with Jesus if I wanted to."*

As soon as he returned to Sunday Mass attendance — and this was all he did for a while — he knew what was missing: the regular contact with God that he needed. After some time he got up the courage to join the youth choir because he liked to sing and had a good voice. It pleased him to see that his singing inspired others and helped them in their prayer. Later his church involvements increased; he joined a book club to expand his formal knowledge of his faith and spirituality.

But what made all the difference for him in terms of his love of God was a weekend retreat he made with several others. The type of retreat he went on is called a "cursillo," which means a "little course" in Christianity. Like the others, he had heard it all before, but the personal witness talks and the shared prayer made what his faith had told him all along suddenly become real and significant. The cursillo "reframed" everything.

He explains, "I learned for the first time in my life that I could have a personal relationship with Jesus if I wanted to. I also discovered how wonderful the Church is, providing us with the precious gifts of the sacraments. And I became aware, to my amazement, that I have been entrusted with a great task to accomplish in my life — to bring the Gospel with me wherever I go and share with others all the riches I've found. In this way I can spread God's Kingdom on earth."

Aaron is faithful to his daily workouts in the gym; now he is also aware of the need to keep in good shape spiritually so he can bring Christ with him into every area of life in which he finds himself. Regular prayer and the reception of the sacraments are key to Aaron. Other tools are daily Scripture reading and the Rosary.

Aaron continues to meet regularly with others who have had the cursillo experience. These meetings are opportunities to share successes and failures in following Christ and to build each other up spiritually.

Aaron's road in life, fortunately, has been without major hurdles. All that was missing for him was making his love for Jesus come alive. But for others the love of Jesus comes as a lifesaving experience. It was so for Steve but, to a far greater degree, the love of Jesus saved the life of a young woman who by some sure instinct of the heart found herself in a convent of the Visitation.

A Second Experience:
Ste. Marguerite Marie Alacoque

Ste. Marguerite Marie grew up in a house of emotional deprivation and tyrannical control. Her father died, leaving five young children. With her mother absent supporting the family, Marguerite Marie experienced what she later described as "continual martyrdom" at the hands of her grandmother, aunt, and great-aunt. She experienced self-loathing and a need for extreme cleanliness, washing her hands many times every day. She described herself as a "sink of vileness."[1]

Her psychological symptoms were compounded by a spirituality that emphasized human sinfulness, especially a horror of impurity in sexual matters. She believed that God's anger could easily be provoked by any transgression. She lived in constant fear of divine thunderbolts and condemnation to hell.

With her emotional and physical health precarious, the family nonetheless succeeded in having her accepted as a nun in the religious family founded by St. Francois de Sales and Ste. Jeanne-Francoise, the Visitandines. It proved to be her salvation. From his image on her wall, St. Francois directed her to follow faithfully all the directives of her religious superiors. She was no longer to punish herself with extremes of penance and other dangerous practices.

One day, in the chapel of the convent, Marguerite Marie received a transforming revelation of divine love. She saw for the first time a Jesus who was no longer her fearsome judge but someone who loved her. This is how she described the experience.

> It seems to me that this is what took place. "My divine heart," he said, "is so inflamed with love for human beings and for you in particular, that being unable to contain it any longer . . . it must spread abroad and manifest itself. . . . I have chosen you . . . for the accomplishment of this great design."[2]

Empowered by this vision of love, she felt herself Christ's own equal, his daughter, friend, and wife.[3] Aware now of her spiritual gifts, her faults and failings seemed of lesser importance. All that was being asked of her was a heart humble and contrite.[4] She became an apostle to the world to proclaim this love.

Jesus assured Ste. Marguerite that anyone who received Holy Communion on nine successive first Fridays of every month would not die without his love. Convinced at last that her unworthiness would not cause her to be cast out and that she could rely upon the divine love, she spread this devotion, which in the years since her death has taken deep root in Catholicism. The devotion to the Sacred Heart of Jesus helped to dispel the idea that only a few chosen individuals merited salvation. Whenever I bring Holy Communion to people unable to come to church I most often do so, as do many priests, on the First Friday of the month. Travelers flying into Paris are presented with a view of the Basilica of Sacré Coeur, built as a reparation to the Sacred Heart of Jesus for the affront of the Great War, World War I. Homes consecrated to the Sacred Heart of Jesus and enshrining his image, though they may be unaware of it, owe this practice to a nun who discovered in Jesus the love she was seeking. Great has been the positive impact of a loveless nun who discovered how much Jesus loved her.

Aaron, Steve, and Ste. Marguerite Marie Alacoque in different ways became convinced of the reality of divine love for them. They discovered that they had "fallen in love with God." Even for a beginner in the spiritual life, such a conviction is the start of the journey toward God.

Part Two

LIFE SITUATIONS

Five

Changing

"The usual purgation and healing, whether of body or of soul, takes place only little by little.... We must not be disturbed by our imperfections."[1]

In the first part of this book we learned five basic principles to guide our spiritual growth. In this second part we will be applying these principles to various life situations: our need to change, which is always ongoing; praying, in which we must be persistent and constant; loving, which needs to express itself in small ways, like observing common courtesies, practicing mutual respect, and making life pleasant for everyone; working, which takes up most of our waking hours; eating, another daily activity that has great spiritual significance; and, finally, resting, the faithful provision for personal renewal that is part of leading a balanced life.

Six spiritual practices allow us to maintain good spiritual health and help us grow in holiness: the Sacrament of Reconciliation, which restores our baptismal holiness when we need forgiveness and healing; daily meditation, an absolute requirement if God's image in us is to become perfect; certain virtues we need to cultivate if our holiness is to become a habit of our being; doing our daily work with diligence; devotion to the Holy Eucharist as our daily bread and model of how to live our lives as a worship offered to the Father with Jesus; and, finally, regular retreats as times to reconnect with our personal goals and to be renewed.

It is necessary to change as we strive more and more to become that person we were consecrated to be when we were baptized: someone who belongs to God alone and who is God's own beloved, just as Jesus is.

When the Gospel was first announced on the day of Pentecost, it had a transformative effect upon its hearers: they were "stricken to their hearts" and asked, "What then must we do?" Peter answered, "You must repent and be baptized in the name of Jesus Christ for the forgiveness of your sins and you will receive the gifts of the Holy Spirit" (Acts 2:3–37).

What is this change called "repentance"? What are we being asked to convert from and to? The Gospel contains the optimistic belief that people can and do change. This changing, though, which is never completed, cannot even begin to happen without God's grace, for we have a limited ability, as our experience tells us, to make change occur. Conversion and the grace of Baptism go together as a single process. The Sacrament of Reconciliation continues the process throughout our lives. The fundamental change we have to undergo is far deeper than an emotional high but occurs at the level of the heart.

The Repentance That Leads to Conversion of Heart

Jesus once said that where our treasure is, there also is our heart (Matt. 6:21). It does us no good to profess faith in God if God is not the highest priority of our lives and at the center of our heart.

For St. Francois de Sales our religious life commences when we bring our faith to heart level and discover God as the treasure we seek. Faith practiced from a heart transformed into love of God is the path of true devotion. St. Francois writes at the start of his *Introduction*, "A man given to fasting thinks himself very devout if he fasts, although his heart may be filled with hatred. . . . Another man thinks himself devout because he daily recites a vast number of prayers, but after saying them he utters the most disagreeable, arrogant, and harmful words at home and among the neighbors. Another gladly takes a coin out of his purse and gives it to the poor, but he cannot extract kindness from his heart and forgive his enemies." Mere "outward actions" that do not come from a transformed heart are "fakes," bogus copies of devotion.[2]

Returning to one's true self is a good beginning definition of conversion. As the most quoted sentence from St. Augustine's *Confessions* explains, "You have made us for yourself, and our heart is restless until it rests in you."[3] Following the path of our deepest desires, finding the ultimate love that our hearts seek, we will encounter God. Conversion is often described as a kind of turning away from lesser loves — the creatures of God — and turning toward God himself. Making God our heart's true treasure and first love is to discover our path to happiness. It is to discard false selves that we may have adopted when, before conversion, we did not know who we were.

Faith that comes from the heart is a major discovery, especially for people like Aaron who were baptized at birth but who for a long time may never have had a personal connection with their beliefs. When faith and our hearts connect, our hearts "burn with the fire of charity,"[4] according to St. Augustine. Using the same image, St. Francois says that once we have embarked upon the path of devotion, the charity that has lain dormant within us "bursts into flames."[5]

We know we have been converted to the life of personal devotion when we find ourselves doing good "carefully, frequently and promptly," with "spiritual agility and vivacity," with "ardor and readiness."[6] These are the words St. Francois uses to describe the new sense of aliveness we feel when we realize we belong to God. We are more focused and energized. Our hearts are truly in it.

Changing: Life Studies

People who are recognized as saints obviously were not born saints. They became saints through many changes over a lifetime. Here are the stories of two men whose lives demonstrate the necessity of ongoing change.

St. Augustine of Hippo

St. Augustine was born in North Africa in 354 and died as the bishop of Hippo in 430. The story of his conversion, the *Confessions*, is, next to the Bible, the most popular book ever written. The world's first autobiography, it is a brilliant philosophical meditation upon the meaning of time and memory. It is also a profound psychological analysis of human motivation, will, and desire; a pioneering theology of sin, conversion, and grace; and a mystical experience of the depths of God. It is also a stunning literary and poetic production.

The *Confessions* takes the form of a letter to God. It does not constitute a "confession" in the sense of an admission of personal sin but a "profession," a testimony of God's grace in Augustine's life. Because he addresses God, Augustine must be totally honest in what he says because God already knows the truth. "Let me confess, then, what I know about myself. Let me confess also what I do not know about myself, since that too which I know about myself I know because you enlighten me."[7]

In the *Confessions* St. Augustine explores two mysteries, the mystery of himself and the mystery of God. He comes to realize the relationship between the two mysteries, for God "is the God of my heart": "I sought for you outside myself, but I did not find you, the God of my heart."[8]

The *Confessions* tells the story of Augustine's life until the age of thirty-three, when he became a Christian and when his mother, Monica, a strong influence in his life, died. He writes from the perspective of ten years later and wonders why, even after Baptism and the grace of ordination as priest and bishop, he is not a better person. His honesty about the continued draw of concupiscence, of his unruly desires and of his old habits, made the Christian apologist Pelagius refuse to recommend the book; it was not the kind of success story he thought would attract others to the faith. Pelagius missed the most central point in Augustine's confession: the presence in his imperfect life of God's transforming grace. That grace had saved him from his messes when his life could have gone in a totally other direction. He shamefully admits dropping the Catholic woman with whom he had lived for fifteen years, the mother of his son, and even trying in his non-Christian days to wean her from her faith. He also tried to separate one of his closest friends from his Christian beliefs. Grace helped to heal him from these personal failings and to live more comfortably with his inner conflicts. Most of all, grace gave him relief from the burden of unhappiness he had been carrying around for years.

Augustine actually recounts two conversions in his life, the first being the discovery of the life of learning that he made at the age of nineteen while reading Cicero's *Hortensius*. The pursuit of truth and the joy of intellectual discussion with like-minded companions became lifelong, nourishing enthusiasms. The second conversion, the one to Christ and to the Church, occurred in the garden of his friend Alypius. He heard a voice — a child's? an angel's? — say, "Pick up and read." What he read was this passage from a scroll of a letter of St. Paul: "Not in rioting and drunkenness, not in chambering and impurities, not in strife and envying;

but put you on the Lord Jesus Christ, and make no provision for the flesh in its concupiscence" (Rom. 13:13–14). It was then that Augustine found at last "a peaceful light streaming into my heart, all the dark shadows of doubt fled away."[9]

> **Grace gave him relief from the burden of unhappiness he had been carrying around for years.**

In his conversion to Christ and the Church, Augustine discovered that the true goal of his life was not just intellectual insight but love, not just wisdom but piety. He found that no writing had much interest for him anymore unless it contained within it the name of Christ.

St. Ignatius of Loyola

St. Ignatius of Loyola (1491–1556), the Basque founder of the Society of Jesus (known as the Jesuits), also exemplifies how a person can change through God's grace.

The Jesuit psychiatrist W. W. Meissner, S.J., notes two pivotal moments in the conversion of St. Ignatius of Loyola: his recovery from a bullet wound in his leg and a nearly psychotic episode in the cave at Manresa. Loyola, who based his self-image on having a successful military career and becoming a romantic hero, found his world crumbling when he suddenly became a disfigured cripple. To restore his previous image he underwent, without anesthesia, two surgeries that we would term cosmetic today. During his lengthy recovery he became acquainted with the lives of the saints and discovered for himself another kind of heroism. Still searching for his new career and thinking it might possibly lie in the conversion of the heathen in the Holy Land, he underwent near personal disintegration in Manresa, a town in Spain. It resembled the radical change undergone by St. Paul when he went from being a persecutor of Christians to becoming the great apostle of Christ. When literally "he fell to the ground" (Acts 9:4) as a result of a vision of Christ, St. Paul had to be led around like a child because he had totally lost his bearing and did not trust his usual reactions and responses (Acts 9:8–9). He had to rebuild himself anew. Similarly, Ignatius discovered that he could shed his previous identity, which turned out to be a false one, and assume a new, truer self. Each became convinced, in his own way, that he was, like Christ himself, God's beloved.[10]

Sometimes this passage, this conversion, is described as going from the "I" to the "Not I." Paul speaks of his experience of it in this very personal way in his letter to the Galatians:

> I have been crucified with Christ, and I live now not with my own life but with the life of Christ who lives in me. The life I now live in this body I live in faith: faith in the Son of God who loved me and sacrificed himself for my sake.
>
> (Gal. 2:19–20)

St. Paul speaks of being crucified with Christ. In many person's lives the means God uses to get our attention is through some kind of wound we sustain that serves as an unexpected jolt, a wake-up call that allows us to be open to God's grace. Our previous illusion of a self-sufficient life has been shattered and we become open to new possibilities for our lives.

In the course of my life as a priest I have met many people whose lives were shaped by some shattering event, whether physical, spiritual, or psychological. They often said, "I am not the same person I once was. I am less than I was and I will never be the same again." And here I respond with an emphatic "No! You are not less than you were, you are more. You will never be the same again, that is true, but you are more."

Applying the Five Spiritual Principles

The first spiritual principle calls for us to start listening to our own hearts, knowing they will not lead us wrong. By listening to our hearts we will discover who we really are. We learn to our amazement and gratitude that we are deeply loved. It is not a love we have to earn for it is given unconditionally as pure grace. We become truly grateful and begin to perceive that life has given us far more than we deserve, whatever our life experience up to now has been.

If we find ourselves still holding on to resentments of any kind, or bitterness or disillusionment, we are still unconverted. No real change can take place, or it will happen for the wrong reason. God truly loves me and finds much goodness in me to love. I have no need to prove my worth.

Because God loves me so much, I want to commit myself totally to him as my first love. I want to resolve by an act of my will to learn God's will for me and follow it out with complete commitment and generosity. I will make the changes that are necessary to bring out more and more the Christ-image given me when I was baptized. Since I belong to God as God's own consecrated child, I want to live up to that new image of myself. This is the second spiritual principle as applied to conversion of life, and it involves my will and requires my commitment.

I know that God loves me and wants to relieve me of all that would oppress my spirit. Christ has told me that once I learn and accept the truth about myself that truth will set me free (John 8:32). I want to own that perfect freedom and I want to rid my life of anything that would deprive me of becoming fully the person

God has made me to be. I want to eliminate all inconsistencies between my present life and the life of Christ. This is the third spiritual principle, striving gently for perfect freedom of heart.

I realize that even though I have committed myself to Christ I still have to live in the sometimes trying and distracting circumstances of my everyday existence. The world does not operate according to the rule of God; this is why I pray every day, "Thy Kingdom come." But even living under less than ideal circumstances I can strive to practice Gospel values and hold on to that perfect peace which is my birthright in Christ. I can still experience joy, and if I am not then I must be doing something wrong. I can and should belong joyfully to God in the midst of all busyness. I must make changes to allow God's joy fully to be mine.

Now I find myself, if I am converted to the Gospel, doing the same things I always did but with a new focus and energy. I love what I do; I do not just endure it. I love it, even the most difficult parts, because I do it all out of love of God. There is so much I want to do and accomplish because I realize God's love given to me even when I least deserved his love. Ordinary tasks that are part of my routine are no longer just routine but new opportunities each day to demonstrate how much I love God. I try to please God in everything I do. I want God to increase and myself to decrease. I want to purify my motives and do all for God's glory and not my own. This is how the authenticity of my conversion will manifest itself according to the fifth spiritual principle: every day, I do ordinary things with great love.

Practicing Holiness:
How to Make a General Confession

St. Francois begins his exposition on change by citing the Bible's love song, the Song of Songs, the parable about the divine lover and the human soul. "The flowers have appeared in our land, the time of pruning the vines has come" (Song of Songs 2:12), says the divine spouse. If we love someone, we will be willing to prune — that is, to make basic changes to more fully enjoy our life together. But more than that, the divine spouse loves us so much that God actually begins the process of "pruning." The pruning becomes a proof of God's special love. St. Augustine at the start of the *Confessions* expresses amazement that God cares for him so much: "What am I myself to you, that you command me to love you, and grow angry and threaten me with mighty woes unless I do?"[11] St. Francois cautions us not to become overzealous in our desire to please the divine lover: we are to proceed step by tiny step, not become discouraged if in our own eyes we are not making sufficient progress, and, above all, remain humble.[12]

The medicine that will purge us of sin is the Sacrament of Reconciliation, which was called confession in the days of St. Francois. He therefore recommends that as the first step in our embarking upon the road of devotion we make what is termed a "general confession," that is, a review of our entire life until then. The aim is twofold: to help us know ourselves before God and to separate ourselves from sin, especially mortal or serious sin. The *Introduction to the Devout Life* discusses how to prepare for and make a general confession. The process includes a second purgation that goes even deeper, the elimination of sinful desires as well as sinful behaviors.

Augustine says that sinners live in "the land of unlikeness." They have become unlike themselves and may even have forgotten who the self truly is.[13] A mortal sin, in the traditional vocabulary used by St. Francois, gravely distorts the divine image in us; a venial sin is uncharacteristic behavior but is not totally disfiguring. Following suggestions made by St. Ignatius of Loyola in his *Spiritual Exercises*, St. Francois lays out ten meditations that will ready us for our general confession. These meditations aim to help us "return to ourselves" — the self that God made that has become deformed through sin.

Like a good physician, Francois prescribes one meditation a day, usually in the morning. The subjects are:

- Our goodness as God's own creature
- The purpose of our life and the elimination of destructive memories
- Becoming more aware of our gifts and developing a grateful heart
- Considering our sins, especially the sin of ingratitude
- Remembering that this is our one and only life
- Living accountably
- The eternal repercussions of everyday actions and choices
- Imagining paradise, the point of arrival of our life
- Taking responsibility for our choices
- Election of the devout life

These meditations intend to place our lives within the horizon of God, the source of all goodness and the goal of our life on earth. They invite us to appreciate and cherish ourselves and to take ownership of our giftedness. They should result in a sense of gratitude; a lack of gratitude for one's life signifies that one is not yet upon the path of devotion. These meditations ready us, according to St. Francois, for general confession.

Among the 150 psalms of the Bible, Psalm 139 (see page 93) stands out as a hymn of praise to God for God's infinite care and concern for each of us, down to the most intimate details of our lives. To the psalmist, God's knowing us "through and through," better even than we know ourselves, is not a cause for alarm; it is profoundly reassuring. God is asked to guide us along the right paths, that we would do nothing to dishonor his handiwork, the "wonder of myself."

St. Francois offers these four pieces of advice about how to make a good general confession:

1. Picture yourself in the presence not of the confessor but of Jesus himself, the gentle savior who wishes to liberate us from our burdens and offers the gift of forgiveness for everything in the past.

2. Open your heart to him, without necessarily labeling anything as sinful or good, for we are forbidden to judge not only others but ourselves. Leave the judgment to God, the merciful and compassionate one.

3. Be candid and sincere, demonstrating great trust and honesty. Change and forgiveness can only come when we are specific and concrete about the things for which we seek forgiveness and which we want to change.

4. Listen to and accept the advice being given you as coming from Christ himself.

After confession, St. Francois advises making three resolutions so that the grace of confession may continue to strengthen us:

- I will return to my life as a son or daughter of the Father given to me on the day of my Baptism.

- I will not dishonor God's image within me but strive always to remember who I am.

- I will consecrate my life to God in its entirety, leaving nothing excluded. These resolutions may profitably be made in writing and read over on a regular basis.

St. Francois gives two cautions. He tells us to remember that even after our conversion our old sinful desires and habits may remain with us. Our daily struggle to overcome them should not discourage us. He also speaks about legitimate pleasures and pastimes, specifically mentioning sports, dancing, the theatre, fine clothes, dining out. While he does not recommend becoming "attached" to them, he does not rule them out either. While we may become truly distressed with our fallen human nature, we cannot redesign ourselves, St. Francois is saying. Let us accept ourselves with all our limitations and even rejoice in our weaknesses, as St. Paul also urges, so that Christ's power in us may be even more manifest (2 Cor. 12:9). By counseling the cautious and thoughtful use of life's pleasures even after our commitment to a life of devotion, St. Francois preserves us from the danger of constructing a false personality. Becoming someone we are not, even for religious purposes, would be spiritual disaster.

PSALM 139

Yahweh, you examine me and know me,
you know if I am standing or sitting,
you read my thoughts from far away,
whether I walk or lie down, you are watching,
you know every detail of my conduct.

The word is not even on my tongue,
Yahweh, before you know all about it;
close behind and close in front you fence me round,
shielding me with your hand.
Such knowledge is beyond my understanding,
a height to which my mind cannot attain.

Where could I go to escape your spirit?
Where could I flee from your presence?

If I climb the heavens, you are there,
there too, if I live in Sheol.

If I flew to the point of sunrise,
or westward across the sea,
your hand would still be guiding me,
your right hand holding me.

If I asked darkness to cover me,
and light to become night around me,
that darkness would not be dark to you,
night would be as light as day.

It was you who created my inmost self,
and put me together in my mother's womb;
for all these mysteries I thank you:
for the wonder of myself, for the wonder of your works.

You know me through and through,
from having watched my bones take shape
when I was being formed in secret,
knitted together in the limbo of the womb.

You had scrutinized my every action,
all were recorded in your book,
my days listed and determined,
even before the first of them occurred.

God, how hard it is to grasp your thoughts!
How impossible to count them!
I could no more count them than I could the sand
and suppose I could, you would still be with me.

God, if only you would kill the wicked!
Men of blood, away from me!

They talk blasphemously about you,
regard your thoughts as nothing.

Yahweh, do I not hate those who hate you,
and loathe those who defy you?
I hate them with a total hatred,
I regard them as mine own enemies.

God, examine me and know my heart,
Probe me and know my thoughts;
Make sure I do not follow pernicious ways,
And guide me in the way that is everlasting.

Six

Praying

"God is in all things and all places. There is no place or thing in this world where he is not truly present.... [God] is present in a most particular manner in your heart."[1]

If you love someone, you want to be in that person's company. In the frequent sharing of our hearts we nourish our relationship and bring our love to deeper levels. Praying is being in God's company and attending to his presence. God is always present; when we feel God is absent, it may mean that we have not been paying enough attention or spending enough time with him in prayer.

It sometimes happens that people who once believed in God — say, as children — find that God is no longer part of their lives. In fact, they may not believe in God anymore. Sometimes people try to resolve their dilemma of unbelief through rational argument, but belief in God is not just a philosophy or a theory — it is a relationship, one that is nourished by prayer. Belief in God is not possible unless we converse with God on a regular basis.

In prayer, God becomes a "you," someone we address and who addresses us. For Christians, this "you" is revealed to be the one we can call "Father" because Christ his only Son has brought us into his unique relationship by giving us his Holy Spirit. Christian prayer, therefore, has a particular structure to it: it is always to the Father, through the Son, in the Holy Spirit. Spiritual masters have found that people who speak of God abstractly have no real relationship with God. God for us is Jesus' Father.

When Ste. Jeanne-Francoise de Chantal asked St. Francois de Sales, as her spiritual director, to describe his experience of prayer, he replied, "It's all so simple and so subtle that one can't say anything about it once it's over."[2] Even though he recommended very specific methods of how to meditate, he also said that the best method to pray is to have no method.

"It's all so simple and so subtle" describes most people's view of what they do when they pray. Jesus himself provided the essential clue to prayer. "When you pray," he taught, "go to a private room, shut yourself in, and so pray to your Father who is in that secret place.... In your prayers, do not babble on ... by using many words" (Matt. 6:5–6). Prayer, in other words, differs greatly from "saying prayers." Prayer comes from our private room, the deepest part of us that only God can understand. One cannot really describe what prayer discloses. It is not just introspection, looking within, an activity that can make us feel burdened and anxious; it puts us in communion with someone larger and greater than our own hearts — it puts us in communion with God.

Those who pray a lot tell us that they can only describe the effect of prayer, not the prayer itself; it can be peacefulness and the feeling of being loved. But sometimes, too, because God's presence is so mysterious, they tell us they often feel nothing.[3] Prayer, then, can be one of our greatest consolations or it can make us aware of how little we are and how little we know. In the latter case, prayer can be the experience of inner desolation and poverty, of an empty place in our hearts that by great discipline we refuse to fill with anything but God. Those who pray tell us that the requisite frame of mind as we come into the presence of God is "lowliness, deep reverence, and trust."[4]

St. Teresa of Avila (1515–82) gives us a "master class" on how to pray from the heart. During the lifetimes of St. Francois and Ste. Jeanne-Francoise, her writings were being translated into French. She had not yet been declared a saint and was simply Madre Teresa at that time, but she was already recognized as someone who helped people go from merely "saying prayers" to "praying." Ordinary people I have met in the course of my ministry as priest and pastor also offer insights on prayer. The five spiritual principles also operate in the realm of prayer, as well as a structure of holiness that St. Francois considers an absolute daily priority, one hour of meditation.

Prayer: A Master Class

The Church recognizes St. Teresa of Avila as the "Doctor of Prayer." With the help of St. Augustine, whose *Confessions* had just become available in Spanish in her lifetime, she came to the new realization that prayer need not be strenuous and prolonged exercises of the mind. Prayer could be something else, something she called *oración mental,* which is, in her words, "nothing else than a close sharing between friends; it means taking the time frequently to be alone with him who we know loves us."[5]

St. Teresa, also known as St. Teresa of Jesus, was one of those remarkable women whose intelligence and spiritual insight could not be confined within the social and religious structures of her time. Entering the contemplative Carmelite order of nuns she reformed it from top to bottom, removing all luxuries and placing prayer at the center of the religious vocation. Teresa founded convents of women and also of men in her reformed order; her life was so filled with activity that her biographer wondered how she could have any time at all for prayer. But this was her secret: prayer was what energized her and allowed her to accomplish so much.

For Teresa, prayer can take place anywhere. "The Lord," she explains, "himself was often among pots and pans, so you can pray to him in the kitchen as well as in the chapel." When Teresa did go to the chapel to pray for guidance, "she had a pretty good idea what God's reactions would be. It wasn't that she expected him to second her own thoughts. It was that, like a trusted longtime servant, she felt she knew what the Master had in mind."[6] This could be described as the goal of prayer, one that Teresa obviously achieved: to reach the point where we and the Lord are one mind and one heart.

St. Augustine opened up many new perceptions for St. Teresa. His description of the soul influenced many others, too, including St. Francois de Sales, who drew upon Augustine's three facets of the human person — memory, intellect, and will — to propose paths in prayer for his directees. Using our intellects to picture a scene in Jesus' life and then to place ourselves in that scene as being addressed personally by Jesus, we proceed in this method of meditation to a holy resolution that will aid in our ongoing conversion to the Gospel way of life.

Teresa of Avila, however, offers a more developed theory of prayer, which includes meditation but is not confined to it. In her autobiography, *Vida*, she uses a very ordinary image from her daily life — the task of watering the convent garden — to illustrate four ways of praying. These four ways of watering the soul in prayer are the well, the water wheel, the stream, and heavy rain.

Those who carry buckets of water from the well to water the garden are the beginners at prayer: they have to use their heads because their hearts are not yet ready to pray. They repeatedly dip buckets into the well for God to fill. This reflects the hard labor of meditating by using our minds to explore religious truths. Determination is the requisite virtue at this stage, because the work is difficult and the rewards are small.

The water wheel, on the other hand, eases the labor of the gardener. With less to do, the soul becomes more focused and rested. Teresa calls this the "prayer of quiet," and it often comes unannounced.

When watered by the stream, the soul needs no human contrivance. God does all the watering of the soul and fills our minds and hearts with great pleasure and satisfaction. Prayer becomes the place where we go in the midst of a busy life for refreshment and comfort. This kind of prayer is accessible to people like Teresa who by circumstance have to live a double life of action and contemplation.

In the heavy rain, we just let God drench us and feel his presence penetrating our existence. It is sheer experience, to be savored for its own sake.

At the age of sixty-two, writing almost nonstop for just a few months, Teresa wrote her masterpiece on prayer, *Interior Castle*. The image of the inner castle or palace comes from the tenth book of St. Augustine's *Confessions*, in which Augustine searches for God by roaming without plan or forethought through the vast spaces of memory. God's presence often cannot be detected in the confusing present or in the unknown future, so Augustine tries to find God by remembering past events where God invisibly, and maybe undetectably, acted in his life. Without trying to control or guide the process, Augustine wanders through the hidden places of memory, allowing everything to emerge.

Teresa describes this memory palace, the soul, as not only large but beautiful, because God has chosen to dwell there, and God can only dwell in beauty. This immense mansion has seven rooms. The first three represent active prayer, in which we do much of the work. The last four represent contemplative prayer, in which God is the principal agent.

The first room, the outermost of the soul, has little light because it is too far from the center whence the light emanates. This room contains a lot of creepy, crawly things that represent our worldly cares and preoccupations. Move out of this room, Teresa advises, as quickly as you can.

In the second room you access sources that can nourish your prayer, like homilies at Mass or good spiritual conversation with friends. You bring these insights into your prayer.

> **The heavy rain is sheer experience, to be savored for its own sake.**

In the next room you begin to put some discipline and order into your life of prayer. You establish routines of prayer, you do penance for your sins and faults, and you seek every opportunity to practice charity.

At a certain point, and almost without notice, you cease trying so hard to pray. You experience God's grace giving you a certain stillness. This is the "prayer of quiet"; you are now in the fourth room.

To describe the fifth room, Teresa uses an image familiar to people living in certain parts of Spain: a silkworm. The tiny silkworm grows by eating mulberry leaves, which come out in summer. Eventually it spins a tent of silk for itself. In this tent it eventually sheds its ugly skin and emerges as a beautiful white butterfly. The silkworm is now so beautiful it does not recognize itself anymore. The silkworm, Teresa explains, is like the soul that has undergone profound conversion: by the grace of God the soul has died to itself and become reborn. But because it is a butterfly, despite its beauty, it is restless and doesn't know where to alight. This is the soul seeking what will ultimately satisfy it.

When we finally become convinced that it is God we have been seeking all along, we have entered the sixth room, the room of betrothal. Augustine's quote is again apt: "You have made our hearts for yourself, O God, and so they are restless until they find their rest in you." But because this is the room of betrothal and the wedding has not yet taken place, even at this stage we can be afflicted — as Teresa herself was at various points — with bouts of depression, illnesses, both physical and mental, and stress in our social relations and in our work.

When we celebrate our marriage to God, we have reached the ultimate room, the very center of our soul. We feel an ease we have never known before, an acceptance of things we never felt capable of, a comfort in our own selves. Christ tells us the words we have been waiting so long to hear: "Whatever is mine is yours; whatever is yours is mine." We find incredible joy in this knowledge. In this most central room God is the soul's spouse and we rest in his embrace.

We should not confuse this stage with a passive withdrawal from the world. On the contrary, at this ultimate point of arrival, we feel new energy and a desire to do great things. We are more alert and capable than ever. No exterior change has taken place in our lives — the same people, the same tasks are there — but everything is different. We react in totally different ways. We deal with things on a different plane. We have come to realize that the most important Being in all the world, the Blessed Trinity, really loves us.

Prayer: Life Studies

We all pray in some form or other and so each of us is, in a way, our own expert in how to pray. Some people say they pray while jogging or on a treadmill or in the shower. The rhythm of running or the splashing of water induce in them a prayerful state. Some pray by sitting and closing their eyes, practicing meditation for an extended period that for them does not feel extended at all. In our parish, we have a "centering prayer" group who meet every Tuesday morning to meditate together. Some people say quick prayers: *Help me. Give me strength. Give me patience. Tell me what to do. Thank you, Lord!* I know an archbishop who says a prayer every time he opens the refrigerator door. "When you live alone," he explains, "you find yourself opening and closing the refrigerator door a lot."

As a pastor, I've learned a lot about prayer by listening to people who pray. One thing is clear: there are many mansions of prayer, and we must find the one where we can meet God. Here are some people who have been my teachers in the ways of prayer.

Chris

Chris is the head of our parish stewardship committee, a group that is learning how to be conscious in the dedication of their time and talent so they can be models for others in the parish to do the same. A money manager by profession and the father of four young children, Chris is a busy man. When his own father died, Chris began to reflect more deeply on what mattered most to him. He came up with only three things that really mattered to him: faith, family, and friends.

Since he has begun learning what the biblical concept of stewardship means as a way of living, Chris did most of the same things he's always done but began to do them as deliberately prayerful acts of adoration and praise of God: to do all for God and to advance the Kingdom of God upon earth.

For example, Chris volunteers every week in his son's elementary school. On the way to the school in his car he says this prayer: "Dear God, I am offering this time in the classroom as my gift to you. I am doing this out of love for you and to achieve your purpose." The effect of this prayer upon Chris has been notable. Instead of doing a volunteer duty as a chore, he now does it as an act of worship and his pleasure in doing it has vastly increased.

In my childhood, I always found taped to the bathroom mirror a "morning offering" my father had placed there to remind him, while he shaved, of how he wished to begin his day. I now realize that, for him, each day offered a new opportunity to serve God and his neighbor.

Louis

For most of his life, Louis was a high-energy entrepreneur. He brought the same energy to music and was a talented drummer in several jazz ensembles. Devoted to God and to his family, he died early from cancer. I walked with him during those final months and saw how his routine of prayer, sustained over many years, gave him the structure and the strength to keep on going cheerfully until the day he died.

Louis was a morning person by temperament. He was always the first up in the morning. He lived near the ocean and, still in his bedclothes and bathrobe, he would sit in his favorite chair facing the ocean to await the sun arising out of the sea. From this same spot each morning, Louis gave thanks to God for the gift of this new day. After spending some time reading a spiritual book and offering spontaneous prayer, he dressed for daily Mass and was ready to begin the day.

Time and place are important when praying, as Louis shows us. Forcing yourself to get up early to pray works only if you are a morning person. Someone else might be most relaxed and alert when the day finally quiets down and the house is still at night. No time is better or more virtuous than another.

When I served as rector of a seminary, I noticed a seminarian sitting on the same bench every day at the same time. He always did his praying there. I asked him about this and he explained that from this one particular place, he could observe the universe. From his bench he could see the subtle changes of seasons and weather — he could detect the presence of God.

Mike

For most of his adult life, Mike suffered from manic depressive psychosis. Never married, although he dated off and on, talented, athletic, sensitive, and compassionate, Mike lost his battle with his illness by ending his life. I shared his suffering through many conversations, and I knew his faith in God.

Mike wrote the following prayer, which brought much comfort to his family after his death. Cryptic and somewhat incoherent, Mike's prayer to God pours out the anguish of his heart and his fervent desire for salvation, a salvation I have no doubt God has given him. Mike's prayer is precious because it expresses a wisdom that was hard won.

God forgave, accept it.
God forgot, out of respect, why don't you.
It's a good idea to forget the past
and stop beating yourself up
over things you can't change.
No more "I should have done this, if only I had done that."
It's okay to learn from our mistakes, but move on.
It's also okay to be a child, not immature,
but make friends with yourself again.
Reconnect, love and be gentle with you.
Be yourself, not some person you think you should be.
Give your care and concerns to God;

He will listen when no one else will.
Don't be angry, possess it, be done with it.
Don't fight with yourself; let the body and mind heal itself,
like a cut on your finger.
If you have lost your soul, one of God's many gifts,
make peace with the Great Creator
and wait patiently for God to lead you back.
Command to love yourself, others, and most of all God
and He will restore you.

Dan

As a game warden, Dan came to appreciate what St. Augustine meant when he said that God wrote two books, not just one. God wrote the Book of Scripture and the Book of Nature, and revealed himself in both.

Dan finds and worships the creator of the heavens and the earth both in church every Sunday and in nature during the week.

Dan also understood the difference between hiking and observing nature that John Muir, founder of Yosemite National Park, often spoke about. Muir thought "hiking" was a vile word and decidedly not the way to experience his beloved Sierra Mountains. For him, "observing" was the proper way to look at nature, observing each individual wildflower, rock, tree. The giant sequoia is to be treated with proper awe and respect, as is each mountain sheep. "Let us permit ourselves," he wrote, "to stand in an idle manner, gaping with our mouths open, demanding nothing, bearing nothing, but hoping and enjoying enormously."

Dan is a permanent deacon, finding and worshiping the creator of the heavens and the earth both in church every Sunday and in nature during the week. Both experiences nourish each other; his meeting with God in what God has made prepares him for the incomparable gift of God's privileged presence in the Eucharist.

Steve

The last example is from Steve. Before Steve had any formal instruction in the Catholic faith, he often spoke with God and received comfort and direction when he needed them.

Steve's prayer is most often the prayer of simple asking, asking the Lord what he should do. He calls it consulting the Holy Spirit who dwells in his heart. "Lord, what would you want me to do? Help me to know your will." This kind of prayer — asking God for what we need — is called *intercessory prayer*. It is the most common form of prayer of those who pray often. It is not at all inferior to other types of prayer, such as praising God or thanking God for his goodness. When we ask God for something directly we are expressing a deep trust in God and God's desire to help us. Jesus commended intercessory prayer very highly.

What Steve gets from his prayer is greater confidence. He compares it to cutting down a tree. Prayer is like the wedge you put in so that the tree falls the right way. As for rote prayers and rituals, Steve tends to regard these as "somebody else's prayers." Part of Steve's continuing development as a Catholic is to connect the Church's prayers with his lived experience so that these prayers truly become his own.

Applying the Five Spiritual Principles

Our spiritual life is all about discovering our own hearts and paying attention to what our hearts tell us. This is the first spiritual principle. We accomplish it through the faithful practice of prayer. Through prayer we learn that we are greatly loved by God and begin to fall in love with God ourselves. In prayer we learn to treasure our being and our fundamental goodness. Through prayer we can experience the fulfillment of our deepest desires because our hearts are inclined to lead us to God, whose presence we learn through prayer.

The problem comes when we finish our prayers and have to attend to the "exterior agenda" — fulfilling all the obligations and expectations placed upon us by the world and by ourselves. To counter the constant pressure of the "exterior agenda" requires great inner strength and firm resolution. We have to commit to living the spiritual life and be willing to follow through on this commitment every day. This is what the second spiritual principle directs us to do: commit ourselves firmly to belonging to God and to no one and nothing else. The spiritual person is a loving person but also someone whom St. Francois describes as "a strong, resolute soul [who] can live in the world without being infected by any of its moods."[7]

Once we commit ourselves to belonging totally to God we notice the need to make certain corrections and changes in the way we live. Prayer helps us recognize these corrections and give us the power to follow through on them. This is the third spiritual principle as applied to prayer — the striving for perfect freedom by removing from our lives all obstacles that are keeping us from God.

Prayer is a delightful exercise but it always has a bottom line — the resolutions we bring back from it into our daily lives. Prayer can serve as our autopilot. As a plane courses across the sky its tendency is to go off course; the autopilot works by constantly bringing it back on course. This is the function of prayer in helping us to achieve and remain in perfect freedom. Prayer involves not just our hearts and minds but also our wills.

Because our existence is one and not broken up into different compartments, we must, according to the fourth spiritual principle, strive to belong joyfully to God even in the midst of all busyness. Prayer will help us to do so, especially if we set aside time at the beginning of our day. By praying early in the morning and soon after rising, we can prepare ourselves for the day's activities. We can think of the day as a gift from God and another opportunity to gain our eternal salvation by the way we live it. In prayer we can anticipate temptations that could lead us astray and so be prepared to avoid them.

Praying in the morning also helps us set the tone for all that follows, giving us a sense of peacefulness and joy that we can return to at idle moments. At the same time St. Francois is realistic and knows we occasionally skip our morning devotions. In those cases he suggests we pray when we can and as long as we can, even if our prayer consists only of a few prayers we have learned by heart.

The fifth spiritual principle urges spiritual integration, doing the ordinary things people do every day, but doing them with a new motivation and energy, and with great love. In this way everything we do becomes a prayer, an offering to God of our entire day. Prayer and activity become woven together into a single piece of cloth. St. Francois said:

> You must even accustom yourself to know how to pass from prayer to all the various duties your vocation and state of life rightly and lawfully require of you, even though they appear far different from the affections you received in prayer. I mean that the lawyer must be able to pass from prayer to pleading cases, the merchant to commerce, and the married woman to her duties as wife and her household tasks with so much ease and tranquillity that their minds are not

disturbed. Since both prayer and your other duties are in conformity with God's will, you must pass from one to the other with a devout and humble mind.[8]

Practicing Holiness: How to Meditate

St. Francois believed that it is helpful for beginners to follow a certain method for meditating, and that meditation should always focus on Jesus and the events of his life. St. Francois's method of prayer was made popular by the writing of Ignatius of Loyola, founder of the then new religious order, the Jesuits.

1. The Preparation

   - Place yourself in the presence of God. Try to clear out your mind of other considerations. Make yourself comfortable and relaxed.

   - Invoke God's presence with a short prayer or mantra such as, "Speak, Lord, your servant is listening" or "Come, Lord Jesus."

2. Meditation

   - Use your imagination to picture an event in the life of Christ, Mary, or one of the saints. Put yourself in that picture so that it is not a past event but something happening to you now. Imagine the words of the Bible being spoken to you personally.

   - Using your mind, try to understand the deeper meaning of the words and how they may apply to your life.

   - Let the meaning of the words touch your heart and open it up to greater trust, generosity, and love.

3. The Conclusion

- Thank God for this experience of his presence.

- Offer your life again to the Father in imitation of Christ's total self-giving.

- Ask for the help you need to put into practice the holy resolutions that have arisen from your prayer.

St. Francois and his contemporaries did not have access to the Scriptures translated into their own language. To nourish and stimulate prayer, therefore, they had to make use of certain books of meditation or pious stories of the life of Christ. We are fortunate not only to have the Bible itself but also the Church's new lectionary and numerous commentaries. If we meditate upon them daily, certain texts will remain powerfully with us and come to mind spontaneously as our everyday experiences remind us of their wisdom and comfort.

St. Francois regarded one hour of daily meditation as essential and placed this practice at the beginning of the second part of his *Introduction,* the part that sets forth practices for the elevation of the soul through a life of devotion. Only later in this part does he even speak of attending daily Mass and say we should make "every effort" to do so.[9] He even allows a "spiritual presence" at Mass if our duties prevent us from being physically present. Nowadays, we may more closely integrate our daily meditation and attendance at daily Mass: we have the rich diet of Scripture in the daily readings of the lectionary. Just reading over the next day's Scriptures and letting them enter our minds is an excellent practice; many Church Fathers used to read the Bible in this way.

Yet just reading the brief portions of Scripture given us in the lectionary does not provide sufficient exposure to its riches. The lectionary allows the Church to relive the life of Christ each year as well as to expose the congregation to all the books of the Bible, but our meditations must take us beyond these excerpts. A contemporary spiritual writer tells us:

> The "short reading" regains its full meaning when situated within a longer, private reading. Now that the temporal cycle gives us snippets, we must take it upon ourselves to read, in the same order, the books of the Bible from which these are taken. Only then will we be able to return to the biblical fullness of the past, even if we cannot (and should not) copy the liturgy of that time.[10]

St. Francois was tolerant of other, more "abstract," ways of doing meditation. His method, he said, was for beginners. He always considered himself a beginner.

Seven

Loving

"Occasions do not often present themselves for the exercise of fortitude, magnanimity, and great generosity, but meekness, temperance, integrity, and humility are virtues that must mark all our actions in life."[1]

In the age of St. Francois, people were discovering anew that the essential component, "the genius," as they called it, of Christianity is love. Loving may seem the most natural thing in the world — to feel love's attraction and succumb to its pull. But love, if we examine it more deeply, requires that our natural inclinations be redeemed and elevated by God's grace if we are to be capable of loving God above all and our neighbor as ourselves. Love is what is most natural to us yet at the same time it is our greatest personal moral challenge. According to St. Francois, love demands the practice of all the other virtues if it is true love and not disguised selfishness. Love is the summary of the Gospel, the essence of the way of devotion, the very nature of God who is love itself (1 John 4:16).

We will examine the nature of love and all that love requires with the holy example of the love of St. Francois and Ste. Jeanne-Francoise for each other serving as a model for the depths and limits of human love. The five spiritual principles also apply to the practice of love, and the daily practice of the "little virtues" can provide a structure of holiness that allows us to put love into action. We all are capable of the grand gesture, the occasional heroism, but the true test of love, St. Francois insists, is the small courtesies and the daily thoughtfulness that demonstrate a love that is sincere.

The Command to Love

The whole Christian message is summarized in the command to love in the First Letter of John. Ste. Jeanne-Francoise, in a letter to someone who also knew St. Francois well, recalled the passage in his *Treatise on the Love of God* in which he wrote that "when charity comes to a soul every other virtue comes with it."[2] This sublime charity, which is purged of every selfish desire, is primarily the love of God for us: "Your love pierced our heart like an arrow" is how St. Augustine described the conversion that allowed him to let go of lesser loves.[3] This love of God for us is mirrored in human love and the sign that we know God is, according to John's First Letter, our ability to love.

> My dear friends, let us love each other, since love is from God and everyone who loves is a child of God and knows God. Whoever fails to love does not know God, because God is love. This is the revelation of God's love for us, that God sent his only Son into the world that we might have life through him. Love consists in this: it is not we who loved God, but God loved us and sent his Son to expiate our sins. My dear friends, if God loved us so much, we too should love each other. No one has ever seen God, but as long as we love each other God remains in us and his love comes to its perfection in us. (1 John 4:7–12)

The person who embarks upon the way of devotion does so out of the amazing awareness of being God's beloved. From all eternity God loved us and willed us into existence. As the supreme expression of God's love for us, God sent his only begotten Son as our savior. This Son, Jesus, eternally remains with us in the Sacrament of the Holy Eucharist, the permanent memorial of his self-giving love on our behalf.

Out of this experience of divine love that is lavish, totally overwhelming, and undeserved, we understand Jesus' new commandment, to love others as he has loved us (John 15:12).

God's love is also made manifest in human love, the love we receive in human relationships. Anyone who has a true friend recognizes the unexpected and undeserved gift. Human love in no way is an obstacle to our love of God or of God's love for us; it is the very manifestation of the kind of selfless bonds that are created between people who know they have been loved by God.

The Gospel teaches that even where there is no mutual friendship, we are able to love even our enemies. Their lack of love for us does not take away our capacity to love them out of the love that we have received from God.

Every time we celebrate the Holy Eucharist we experience God's love all over again in the most concrete way: there is no greater love than this, to lay down your life for your friends (John 15:13). When Jesus called his disciples "friends" and not servants, he elevated their relationship to a new level. They became more than just master and disciples. The sign that they had become friends was that Jesus revealed to them, as friends do, everything about himself and what the Father had taught him (John 15:14–15).

A Christian is one who, every day, does everything, even the most ordinary thing, out of great love.

The Love of St. Francois de Sales and Ste. Jeanne-Francoise de Chantal

Both St. Augustine and St. Francois placed a high value on human friendship. The friendship of Ste. Jeanne-Francoise and St. Francois, which endured for nineteen years, is one of the most exemplary in Christian history. To see their respective tombs side by side in the Basilica in Annecy is to visualize their eternal love for each other in God and how they became forever no longer two souls but one: "notre âme" — "our soul" — as St. Francois described it.[4]

The love of these two saints for each other was a means to their personal holiness, a "bond of perfection." It was also a love that was extraordinarily fruitful in the religious families that they founded together. How they managed their relationship over many years provides an insight into how a love that is both human and divine can become purer and more mutually enriching with the passage of time.

At the age of twenty Jeanne Fremyot married the Baron de Chantal, with whom she was deeply in love. Their marriage ended tragically when the baron was killed in a hunting accident. This left Jeanne a widow with children to raise. She was still overwhelmed with her loss when St. Francois came to her native city of Dijon to preach a Lenten series of sermons; he was thirty-seven and she was thirty-two. Their mutual esteem and affection were immediate.

An intense correspondence between them began immediately. St. Francois kept all her letters to him and annotated them. She kept all his letters as well and these were later published. She burned her letters to him after his death.

As he was ending his sojourn in Dijon on April 26, St. Francois had this brief note passed to Ste. Jeanne-Francoise: "God, it seems to me, has given me to you: I am more strongly confident about it, hour by hour. This is all I can say."[5]

At the time they met, Ste. Jeanne-Francoise was under the spiritual direction of a priest who was not helping, but actually exacerbating, her spiritual struggles. The protocol of the time required that no one dare intrude into the confidential bond of director and directee. At this early stage in their friendship, St. Francois and Ste. Jeanne-Francoise were striving to find a way for her out of this stifling relationship. The first note he wrote her suggests that God was giving St. Francois to her for this service.

> **The love of these two saints for each other was a means to their personal holiness.**

Within a week, St. Francois began the first letter of his correspondence by writing, "It is with the intention of giving you even more assurance that with due consideration I observe my promise to write to you as soon as I could. The more I am separated from you externally, the more I feel joined to you interiorly."[6]

Six letters, most of them lengthy, came from St. Francois before the year was out: May 4, June 14, June 24, October 14, November 21, and December 2. In the same period he also wrote to Ste. Jeanne-Francoise's brother, André Fremyot, on the subject of preaching. This letter was later reproduced as a pamphlet and became well known. It contains the phrase adopted by John Cardinal Newman as his motto, "le coeur parle au coeur" ("cor ad cor loquitur," "heart speaks to heart").[7]

His next letter to Jeanne-Francoise, while attempting to set her scrupulous mind at ease about consulting him in addition to her present spiritual director, defines their relationship as "Christian friendship." St. Francois admits that he has a lively and extraordinary desire to be of service to her spiritual life and says he believes this desire comes from God: "God has given me to you," he declares. Significantly, he does not say, "God has given you to me," which would imply that she is to satisfy his own need for intimacy, but rather that God wishes him to be of some spiritual service to her. He then gives his definition of Christian friendship, drawing upon the Letter of St. Paul to the Colossians.

In this Epistle Paul uses the imagery of clothing and says he should wear the garments of compassion, generosity, humility, gentleness, and patience as well as forgiveness. This particular passage must have been a favorite of St. Francois because he frequently highlights these virtues in living the Christian life every day. "Over all these garments," St. Paul adds, "put love, which is the bond of perfection" (Col. 3:14). St. Francois writes:

> Again I must say to you, in order to carve a path for all the responses that could form themselves in your heart, that I never intended that there be any bond between us which would carry with it any obligation except that of charity and true Christian friendship. This bond St. Paul has spoken of as "the bond of perfection," and truly it is that, for it is indissoluble and can never be released. Every other bond is temporary, even the vows of obedience which are broken at death and by many other circumstances. But the bond of charity grows over time and takes on new power over a long duration. It is exempt from the rupture of death whose scythe cuts down all except charity. "Love is stronger than death and more lasting than hell," Solomon has said. There, my good Sister (and permit me to call you by this name, which is the one by which the apostles and first Christians expressed their intimate love for each other), there is our

bond, these are our chains which, the more they restrain us and weigh down upon us, the more they give us ease and freedom. This power is but sweetness, their violence only smoothness; nothing is so flexible and nothing more solid. Consider me then intimately bound to you and don't worry yourself except to know that this bond is not in opposition to any other bond, whether of religious vows or marriage vows. Live then entirely at peace with this matter. Obey your first spiritual director with filial devotion and freedom, and avail yourself of my direction with charity and frankness.[8]

The basis of their lifelong association, "Christian friendship," is something of God, based upon charity, a supernatural virtue, but also based on a tender and mutual attraction. These two are not opposed; in fact, together they are conducive to the eternal salvation of each partner.

"God's love is very willing that we have other loves," St. Francois writes in his *Treatise*. He continues:

Nor can we easily discover which is the chief love of our heart, for this human heart often draws most affectionately into its complacency the love of creatures; yes, on many occasions it makes the acts of its affection for the creature far more numerous than that of its love for its Creator. Yet all the time sacred love does not cease to excel all other loves.[9]

In his development of the notion of "Christian friendship" St. Francois owes much to St. Augustine, for whom friendship was a central spiritual reality. "Without friends, I could not be happy," Augustine admits, "but I have loved them for their own sakes."[10] Augustine defined a friend as "my second self: one soul dwelling in two bodies."[11] For Augustine, lust is a violation of the boundaries of friendship.[12] Perhaps, like Plato, Augustine believed that celibacy could only increase the level of friendship's communication.

But by declaring that "God's love is very willing that we have other loves," St. Francois proves himself an innovator in the Christian spiritual tradition. Not a few Christian writers have regarded all human relationships as a distraction from the primary love we owe to God alone. In making such a claim, St. Francois would say, they have naively assumed that anything like the pure love of God alone could exist all by itself in any human heart.

For years Ste. Jeanne-Francoise and St. Francois met on a regular basis to discuss both matters concerning the religious congregation they had founded and the condition of their own souls. Before their final meeting, however, in October 1622 in Lyons, three years had passed since they had seen each other. Part of the reason was the busyness of their lives, but mostly this separation was the result of St. Francois having told Ste. Jeanne-Francoise in May 1616 that from now on she should not rely upon him but upon "God alone." In that exchange Francois had emphatically commanded Ste. Jeanne-Francoise to strip herself of all human supports and to present herself naked in her neediness before God.[13] In her response, one of the rare letters of Ste. Jeanne-Francoise to survive, she writes:

> I am greatly pleased with these instructions as well as the one that insists that you guard your solitude, for it will be used in the further service of your dear spirit. I could not say "our" because it seems to me that I no longer have any part of it now that I find myself so denuded and stripped of all that was most precious to me.
>
> My God! My true Father! How deep the razor has cut![14]

Their relationship, so long established and still as committed, had moved to another plane, one in which St. Francois wished to remove some of its ambiguities. When they met three months before his death on December 28, Ste. Jeanne-Francoise had come with two lists, one that related to the state of her own soul, the other to the religious congregation. St. Francois began the exchange.

"My Mother, we have several free hours. Which one of us should begin?"

"Me, please, my Father," Jeanne quickly replied. "My heart greatly needs to be attended to."

His response showed untypical impatience about her presenting her private concerns: "What, my dear Mother? Do you still have urgent desires and personal choices? I thought I would find you quite angelic." Then he added, "We speak about ourselves [when we are] in Annecy; now we should attend to the business of our congregation. How much I love our little Institute because God is loved so well there."[15]

Wendy Wright gives us Ste. Jeanne-Francoise's reaction.

Without a word Jeanne folded up the sheet of paper on which she had made some notes for her review of conscience and unfolded the larger sheaf of papers which contained the information necessary for a discussion of the order's affairs.[16]

In 1627, five years after the death of St. Francois, Ste. Jeanne-Francoise gave her testimony in the process that would eventually lead to his canonization as a saint. This testimony remains the most accurate and lively biography of the saint. The fact that he was not canonized in her lifetime was one of the greatest disappointments she had to endure. In the *Testimony*, Ste. Jeanne-Francoise says of her friend:

For my own part, from the time I first got to know him, which was when he preached the Lenten sermons at Dijon in 1604, I admired him as an oracle. I called him a saint in my heart and that is what I really thought he was. Seeing that I had described him as a saint in one of my letters, he asked me to stop this and he pointed out that holy Church hadn't endowed me with the power to canonize saints. My veneration for him was such that I used to kneel down to open and read his letters; I kissed them in a spirit of reverence and devotion, taking what he said to me as coming from the Spirit of God.[17]

She summarized her feelings by stating to the canonization inquiry, "For my part, God had given me such a high regard for him that I would gladly have been the humblest servant in his house to have the joy of watching him and listening to his holy conversation, for he radiated holiness in all he said and did."[18]

His regard for her was at the same level of admiration and affection. Although she was technically under his spiritual direction, the benefit of their friendship was mutual. She claimed that his masterpiece, the *Treatise on the Love of God,* was an unconscious self-portrait of its author,[19] but Henri Brémond is also correct in observing that it was "for her and near her that this book was written; what is more, it is of her and the first Visitandines that it tells."[20]

Applying the Five Spiritual Principles

If we know our hearts deeply, we recognize that its first attraction is for God, the God of our hearts, the One who made our heart for himself alone. But, as St. Francois teaches, God's love allows many other loves. Being loved by God expands our heart: we increase our love's sweep to include everyone. Our love of others does not diminish our love of God but is a true expression of it.

The second spiritual principle requires that by an act of the will we strive to make God the center of our lives and nothing else. God must be our treasure, our highest priority. To do this, if we follow the third spiritual principle, we must strive to free our love of entangling dependencies. To be free of all dependencies is a lifelong task and we should be gentle with ourselves if even after much effort we find ourselves falling back into old patterns in our relationships. The key is not to give up in our daily struggle to love God above all.

Every life knows loneliness. Even the most happily married experience the ultimate loneliness of knowing a void that only God can fill. True joy will come not by running away from the void through hyperactivity and other distractions but by staying faithful to God in prayer. This is the fourth spiritual principle.

The fifth spiritual principle calls to our attention the many daily opportunities we have to show love to each other. The ordinary courtesies we extend, the patience we display with human imperfection, the encouraging words and gestures we make are all ways of showing a love that is not feigned.

Practicing Holiness: Practicing the Small Virtues

The third part of St. Francois's *Introduction to the Devout Life* is a series of instructions on the practice of virtue. Virtues are habits of being that give shape to our character and allow us to deal with prosperity and adversity with strength and resilience. The highest of the virtues are the "theological" ones, that is, those virtues that are beyond our capacity to cultivate by ourselves and are divine gifts: faith, hope, and charity. St. Francois does not neglect these, but gives most space to those virtues that make our social relations easy and pleasant.

The so-called "small virtues" are the everyday courtesies and thoughtfulness that bring supernatural charity down to earth. Doing everyday, ordinary things out of great love is a founding principle of the spiritual life; practicing the small virtues offers the greatest possibilities for its implementation.

In the Beatitudes Jesus elevated what might be called small virtues to supreme importance in the practice of the Gospel. Gentleness, meekness, humility of heart, which are the opposite of aggression and self-promotion; purity of heart and of intention, which admits no hidden agenda in our relationships; mercy, kindness, the willingness to forgive; peacemaking and the ability to reconcile differences — these, Jesus says, are the qualities and attitudes that bring us blessedness in this world and in the Kingdom of God (Matt. 5:3–12).

The practice of the small virtues may seem far inferior to the high demands of perfection the Gospel requires. St. Francois insists, however, that becoming a good enough human being is no small goal: it is the first and indispensable step toward holiness.

St. Francois also calls attention to the practice of virtues that are essential to our own way of life and personal vocation.

In practicing the virtues we should prefer the one most conformable to our duties rather than one more agreeable to our tastes.... Every state of life must practice some particular virtue. A bishop's virtues are of one kind, a prince's of another, a soldier's of a third kind, and those of a married woman are different from a widow's. All men should possess all the virtues, yet all are not bound to exercise them in equal measure. Each person must practice in a special manner the virtues needed by the kind of life he is called to.[21]

These virtues, if we cultivate them actively, will make our everyday life our own way to salvation.

Sometimes individuals may feel called to cultivate a virtue they think they need or they wish to be known for. St. Francois commends such a focus because, he believes, by the perfect practice of a single virtue a person can reach the heights of all virtue.[22] He mentions the example of St. Louis, who, while king of France, visited hospitals and with his own hands tended the sick as if serving for pay.[23] For another person, just striving to complain less about life's inevitable inconveniences and disappointments can bring great personal benefit.[24] As for himself, St. Francois focused on the practice of humility both in his outward behavior toward others and in his interior disposition. Being a bishop with royal connections in a small, remote diocese, he knew how easy it would be for him to treat others with condescension if he did not strive in every way to be the humble person he wished himself to be.

"Small virtues" are the everyday courtesies and thoughtfulness that bring supernatural charity down to earth.

One day Steve and I discussed what makes a marriage work. As a mature man married to a professional counselor, Steve has learned a lot about the constant effort it takes to keep love alive.

Steve spoke about mutual admiration and respect. I knew exactly what he meant. Living closely with someone, you become aware of their flaws and oddities, but if your relationship is to flourish you must look beyond them to appreciate the uniquely gifted person with whom you have the privilege to share your life. The word "respect" comes from a Latin word that means "to look at": if you love someone, you look at that person always with loving eyes.

Time together, Steve said, is also at the top of the list. Some busy couples resort to setting up dates to be together on a regular basis. This may seem extreme, but given all the demands upon people's time, it is actually a practical way to make sure the time together really happens. Spending time together often requires the sacrifice of precious leisure time, when we could be doing other things we like. The commitment to time together demonstrates love in a way that other things like gifts cannot equal.

Having come later to the Catholic faith, the religion of his wife, Steve sees this faith commitment and the values that go with it as strengthening the bond of his love. Steve and Margarete can work for the same things in life because they share a conviction about what is important to them both.

Steve recognizes that Margarete has brought much to his life that has helped him greatly. The mutual sharing of gifts and mutual support with unconscious generosity is one of the fruits of being in love.

In his last comment about what love requires, Steve mentioned "space." He and Margarete recognize that they need time alone. As mature people they are not threatened by not being constantly in each other's company, nor are they jealous of how this time apart is spent. Time alone can mean time with God, our primary lover, God who gives us the grace that energizes all our other loves and purifies them of self-seeking.

Eight

Working

"Imitate little children who with one hand hold fast to their father while with the other they gather strawberries or blackberries from the hedges. So too if you gather and handle the goods of this world with one hand, you must always hold fast with the other to your heavenly Father's hand and turn toward him from time to time to see if your actions or occupations are pleasing to him."[1]

Aaron made a remarkable spiritual breakthrough on a weekend retreat at a critical time in his life. Among his newly discovered insights was the amazing realization that God was entrusting him with a great work, to bring the Gospel with him wherever he went and to transform that place through his personal witness to Gospel values. Chris, before doing something as ordinary as volunteering in his children's school, offered that activity to God as a conscious act of worship. Both Aaron and Chris experienced new energy and personal satisfaction in doing the things they ordinarily do but doing them as part of their contribution to a great project, bringing God's Kingdom to the earth. In the Lord's Prayer, we pray, "Thy Kingdom come! Thy will be done on earth as it is in heaven!" We play a large part in bringing God's Kingdom to the earth by our work, which has a deep spiritual component.

Spirituality has often been mistakenly thought of as a leisure-time activity. Indeed, there has been an enduring tradition in

Christianity of elevating the practice of contemplation, which requires extended periods of leisure, over what was called "action," the burden of work. There was also the mistaken idea that since our true home is in heaven we should concentrate our spiritual efforts on assuring our eternal salvation there and not concern ourselves with the affairs of this world.

Within such a worldview, laypeople really couldn't have much of a spiritual life. The best they could do, it seemed, was to ask the religious professionals — priests and religious — to pray for them, since they had little time to pray themselves.

In our age, working takes up most people's time. For economic reasons women and men must find employment outside the home. If the work people do has no spiritual meaning, then most people's lives are deprived of any religious significance.

The Second Vatican Council (1962–65) directly addressed this issue. It was the first ecumenical council in the history of the Church to speak of the mission and vocation of laypeople. We will sketch out a "spirituality of work" according to which our engagement in everyday activity can be both a means to our personal salvation and a contribution to the building of God's Kingdom here on earth. St. Francois's teaching laid much of the groundwork for the insights of the Second Vatican Council. His life also showed how hard it is to achieve the proper balance between action and contemplation. The five spiritual principles apply to our working life; a structure of holiness can be provided by respecting our human limits and exercising moderation in our work.

The Spiritual Meaning of Work

According to the Second Vatican Council there is no two-tiered holiness, one for the religious and the other for the laity. All are called to one and the same perfection, but by different routes.

Upon everyone who is baptized — religious or lay — are conferred the threefold messianic offices of Christ: to be priest, prophet, and ruler. The laity exercise these offices specifically by their engagement in secular realities. In their priestly role laypeople praise God in the midst of the world, becoming the voice of all creation in giving glory to their creator. They are to offer to God all that they do in their secular professions and occupations as a great act of worship that is their whole life. In their role as prophets, they can make Christ known to others, especially by the way they live out the virtues of faith, hope, and love every day. By transforming from within that part of the world for which they are responsible, the laity exercise their role as Christlike rulers or shepherds. Like leaven in bread and light from a candle, laypeople help bring about God's rule of the earth through their own personal contributions in their daily work.

The Council also raised the deeper question of how much any one human being can do, no matter how dedicated and talented, to bring about God's Kingdom on earth. How many well-intentioned people, after a lifetime of generous effort, have felt themselves defeated by the great problems of the world that they tried in vain to solve? The environment needs to be saved for future generations. Businesses should be run according to ethical principles and should not oppress the poor. War must be averted and peace should reign. But what can we do about these things? We can ally ourselves with God; we can see what God is doing and try to do it ourselves. In the end the coming of God's reign will be accomplished only by God, but we can make a contribution to that cause, in fact a crucial one.

What precisely is the human contribution? The Second Vatican Council responds in a beautiful way that does not dissolve the mystery that is behind this question. It teaches that in God's future Kingdom we will find again all our good deeds and selfless acts, but "purified and elevated."[2] Nothing that we have done for the good, no matter how small, will be lost.

Pope John Paul II, following along the Council's lines, has developed what he calls the "gospel of work." All people, he says, should evaluate the work they do according to three criteria. First, it should be more than just a job; it should be a vehicle for our self-fulfillment and personal growth. Second, we should be able to take pride in what we do, performing our tasks with honesty and integrity. Third, the work itself should be of benefit to humanity and allow us time to devote to our families and to leisure.

> *Religious people see the life they*
> *have been given as a personal*
> *calling from God.*

There are many jobs, as we well know, that do not provide much opportunity for self-fulfillment or personal growth. The pope knows this, too. He goes on to say that the work people do should not define their worth but that the human persons doing the work bring dignity and value to that work, no matter how menial it is. If the worker brings a supernatural perspective to the workplace, trying to serve God and society there, that person elevates the work into something of eternal value. By doing so, the working person is saved from three possible dangers. One is succumbing to a materialistic outlook, working just for the money and the personal comforts money buys. The second is conformity, mindlessly accepting the prevailing values and lifestyle of the culture in which we live. Spiritual lethargy, a careless attitude, is the third danger — just going through the motions but really giving up.

That having been said, there is no need to romanticize our daily challenges and difficulties in the workplace. Recall that in the

Book of Genesis, after the world lost its condition as paradise, work became a burden, something we have to do with the sweat of our brows. The oppressiveness of our daily routine can be redeemed if we unite what we do with the sufferings of Christ upon the cross for the salvation of the world.

Religious people see the life they have been given as a personal calling from God, a vocation that, if followed faithfully, will lead to personal salvation. In fact, we speak of a threefold vocation that each of us has from God. The first, most fundamental calling is to be a baptized child of God with all the personal dignity, rights, and duties that come with such a royal status. Within that baptismal call is the vocation to a particular state in life as married people or celibates, religious or laity, and to the job we perform for our livelihood. The third vocation embraces all the personal gifts and unique qualities each of us brings to these other two, endowing them with our own unique contribution. I have found helpful the motto our parish stewardship committee came up with to describe how each of us should own and be responsible for all the gifts God has entrusted to us: Find yourself doing God's work. When we do God's work, in other words, we "find" ourselves, our true life's vocation.

Work in the Life of St. Francois

St. Francois provides both an inspiriting example of someone who loved and was successful at his work, and a cautionary tale about someone whose excessive zeal cost him dearly.

Our best source for a true appraisal of St. Francois in his working life as a bishop and pastor is Ste. Jeanne-Francoise's *Testimony*. Given in evidence in the official investigation of his saintliness, it contains many sharp details and acute insights. She cites a letter from Francois to herself in which he confides, "O how consoling

and honorable I find the service of souls!"[3] This statement is ver-
ification that Francois found his true vocation in the work he was
doing. He enjoyed what he did and bore its burdens with equa-
nimity. He also realized that his work changed him in significant
ways, making him a better person. "When I was anointed bishop,"
he wrote in another letter to Jeanne-Francoise, "God took me to
himself and away from my own self, and then he gave me back to
my people, that is to say, he changed me from being something
in my own right to being something that existed only for their
sakes."[4]

The same comment that St. Francois makes about himself in
the celibate life has been made to me by countless married people.
They say that if they had never married and had children they
would have been far more self-centered than they are, spending
their time acquiring things that would give them pleasure rather
than fulfilling the demands that come with being in a family.
Work, in other words, can deepen our Christian conversion.

"Zeal" is how those who knew him best described St. Francois's attitude toward work. But often our vices are nothing more
than our virtues carried to excess. This was certainly true for
St. Francois: his zeal often — too often — tipped into overwork.
He frequently lost the balance that he was always striving to
achieve. The result was danger to his health and to his spiritual
life. Ste. Jeanne-Francoise said:

> Many people believe, and I am one of them, that he wore
> himself out and shortened his life by this devoted and loving
> service, for he often neglected meals and sleep because of it;
> he suffered hardship and toil which no one else could have
> stood, and this I really know. He said we must never refuse
> our neighbor the good and comfort it lies in our power to
> give him. When people tried to explain to him that he could

not go on toiling like this for long and that he was damaging his health, he answered calmly that ten years more or less just did not matter.[5]

Jeanne-Francoise also is insightful about the harmful effects his overwork had upon his spiritual life. In the last phase of his life lasting several years he could find little time for prayer, she says, because his work took over everything. One day she challenged him as to whether he had prayed and he admitted he had not, but said that working and praying are all the same thing anyway. She puts a positive spin on this by noting that his work was an "uninterrupted prayer" and that in all he did he never lost his union with God.[6] His comment, however, could be read another way — that working and praying being the same thing, he was not giving enough time to prayer. This is a dangerous posture.

From time to time, especially later in life, St. Francois consoled himself by fantasizing about retirement. He would live in a chalet in the Swiss mountains, say his Rosary, and meet the occasional visitor. That time never came. He died of a stroke at the age of fifty-five.

The fact that even a saint could not achieve perfect balance in life should encourage rather than discourage us. God's Kingdom is still not here and the world runs according to its own rules which, despite our best efforts, have harmful effects upon us all. It is the effort that counts, not the success.

What St. Francois stressed was not perfection but flexibility. I once gave a retreat to some very oppressed people — directors of parish religious education programs. During the conferences, some busied themselves making Rosaries. One of the retreatants, lamenting her lack of time to pray, said, "My Rosary should have only one bead — a one-bead Rosary." St. Francois would have immediately understood.

Applying the Five Spiritual Principles

As Steve reflected with me on his life as a working man, I could see how he was rediscovering, through his life experience, the spiritual principles that St. Francois articulated. Steve loved doing masonry. It was something he did, and did well, since his youth. Working with natural materials was congenial to his spirit, and the physical task allowed his mind to be free to meditate, even if he didn't call it that at the time. When his stepfather became ill and he was put in charge of the company, he stopped doing the physical work and confined himself to supervision and management. His aim became not to produce something beautiful he could be proud of but to make money. His world eventually collapsed from overwork, too much responsibility, and his addiction to alcohol, which deadened his heart's pain. When seeking employment later in life to support himself and his family, Steve consciously paid attention to what his heart was telling him — the first spiritual principle — and it led him to a form of employment that is much more satisfying for him.

I am always impressed with Steve's willpower, the strength of will that he exercises to keep his life in balance and to avoid falling back into old patterns of thinking and acting. The commitment part of the spiritual principles is central to Steve's present life.

The third spiritual principle stresses gentleness with our own spirits as we strive for perfect freedom of heart. Here Steve has further work to do, or rather, less work and effort and more patient acceptance of imperfection in himself and others. Anger has always been an issue with Steve and so becoming less hard on himself may help him to lower his level of frustration. In the past he had a fairly active social life, partying every weekend and sometimes during the week. Nowadays he is content to stay at home more than he did and to savor the blessings of his life.

Steve knows that if his spiritual life is going to be successful he must bring it with him everywhere. The fourth spiritual principle sets a test: if we can handle the ordinary stresses associated with our daily tasks with a measure of joy, then God is truly present at every moment of our lives.

At one time, between his masonry work and his present job as a real estate appraiser, Steve worked in a youth alternatives program. The work was draining and didn't pay very much. His co-workers seemed to be constantly in a state of depression because society obviously did not value their services by paying them a salary comparable to other, less demanding, jobs. They may have gone into this work of helping troubled youth with high motivation but, like Steve, they often thought of themselves as "bleeding hearts." What they needed to do, as the fifth spiritual principle teaches, is to do all that they do not for the money or the recognition but simply out of love. Love sets the standard for self-worth, love and nothing else.

Practicing Holiness:
Working for the Kingdom of God

St. Francois could not have anticipated the profound critique of present social arrangements and institutionalized injustice that have characterized modern church social teachings. He was more comfortable counseling the practice of charity and the works of mercy than he was preaching a more just society. Work for him was a human necessity that could be offered up, not something that might manifest human creativity and serve to bring about God's kingdom upon the earth. But nonetheless he did provide a fundamental spiritual principle that has aided social activists like Dorothy Day ever since, and that is, "little by little."

In the *Introduction to the Devout Life*, St. Francois recognizes that "the mountain of Christian perfection is very lofty" and we might be tempted to ask, "How will I be able to climb it?" To this he replies, "Little by little." In the spiritual life as well as in the field of social justice and any other human endeavor, we must respect the human scale, do things "little by little" and not be discouraged; otherwise we could head for disaster. Was not the first human sin recorded in the Bible the sin of attempting to "be as gods" (Gen. 3:5)? Practicing the small social virtues, doing individual acts of kindness — these may not seem to mean too much in terms of the intractable problems the world is facing, but if they are done in union with God the results are literally beyond calculation. Robert Ellsberg used this Salesian principle as the title for his collection of the writings of Dorothy Day: *By Little and by Little.*

Every working person who does the work consciously as a Christian endows that work with spiritual value. This can be done if we strive to go against the pull of the media and other forces and live humbly, honestly, and on a more human scale that doesn't require us to work excessively just to sustain an overly elevated way of living and consuming. We keep this spiritual perspective also if we see our work as an opportunity to serve the world, trusting in God's personal love for us and listening always to the voice of the Holy Spirit in our hearts. In this way our work can be a satisfaction.

Though our human contribution to the coming of God's kingdom on earth may be little, its effects can be incalculable if we align our work with God's. Here are four suggestions as to how to do so.

We should strive, first of all, not to separate our relationship with God and with our family, our professional and social life, but unite them into one single existence. We must not succumb to the danger of separating our ordinary life from our religious life. We should be recognizable as the same people on Monday that we are on Sunday; we should display no inconsistencies, have no separate compartments. We should be the same person in our family, profession, and social activity.

Because God can be found everywhere, at every moment of the day and night, we must bring this supernatural vision to everything we do. Our everyday life opens itself up into eternity if we strive every day to work out our eternal salvation by offering all to God.

> **We must respect the human scale, do things "little by little" and not be discouraged.**

We should see as our great task lifting the whole world to God and transforming it from within. Jesus taught that we are to be the salt of the earth and the light of the world. This is the incentive, the motivation that should drive us. Far from distracting us from our earthly tasks, our Christian faith gives us greater reason to engage in politics, education, the law, medicine, and all other worthwhile endeavors because we see our efforts as helping God's reign to come.

But fourth, and most importantly of all, we must pray. The world in the end will be redeemed not just by our work but by our prayer. Prayer first and last. By praying we will be helped to do the right things, to act thoughtfully, and not to do more harm than good. It is prayer that will help us to keep to the principle of "little by little," the mustard seed principle according to which a small human contribution by the power of God can grow into the largest of bushes.

St. Francois gave us the image of children picking berries, one hand doing the work, the other in their father's hand. As we do our work, the saint is saying, we need to turn from time to time to our Father, whose hand is joined to ours, to see if what we are doing is truly pleasing to him.

Nine

Eating

" ... the Mass, center of the Christian religion, heart of devotion and soul of piety, the ineffable mystery that comprises within itself the deepest depths of divine charity, the mystery in which God really gives himself and gloriously communicates his graces and favors to us."[1]

Soon after the Metropolitan Museum of Art in New York City created a new installation of Byzantine art, I had the opportunity to examine a number of the implements for eating used in the Byzantine period. I was struck by the elaborate religious symbolism that adorned each cup, spoon, and plate. It was clear that for Christians of that time the act of eating was no mere secular activity; it was a prayer-filled daily ritual, an occasion to be reminded that Christ himself is the hidden host at every meal we take. In the Gospels, we read that Jesus took many meals with a wide variety of people. In the Gospel according to St. John he was the actual but unacknowledged host at the wedding feast of Cana in Galilee. His presence and that of Mary his mother allowed the guests to enjoy the best vintages in unlimited quantity. Fasting from food is an essential element of Gospel living, but fasting is inappropriate when we are privileged to be in the company of the heavenly bridegroom. The act of eating itself, like every other ordinary daily activity, is loaded with spiritual significance.

"Happy are those who are called to his supper"

Jesus once suggested that we imagine heaven as a festive banquet to which we all are invited. He did not find it irreverent to compare the experience of delightful dining with what it will be like to live in the eternal presence of God. Jesus himself lingered over many meals and did not consider this activity unimportant. Much of his teaching, in fact, took place over meals. After his resurrection he even prepared a meal himself for his startled disciples upon the shore of the lake where they had been fishing through the night. "Come and have some breakfast," he said (John 21:12). It was perfectly natural, in light of all the meals they had had together while he was on earth, that Jesus chose a meal as the sacrament of his continuing presence among them. "Do this in memory of me" was his command at the last festive meal they enjoyed (Luke 22:19). Eating is a fundamental human activity and in these many ways Jesus revealed the spiritual nature and transcendent meaning of so humble and ordinary an act.

Dorothy Day is famous for having lived a life of voluntary poverty in the most affluent country in the world. Yet even she did not find any contradiction between well-prepared food and simplicity of life. In a particularly vivid entry in her journal, she expresses her disdain for carelessly prepared meals.

> We had hard baked potatoes for supper, and overspiced cabbage. I'm in favor of becoming a vegetarian only if the vegetables are cooked right. (What a hard job cooking is here! But the human warmth in the dining room covers up a multitude of sins.) Another food grievance: onions chopped up in a fruit salad, plus spices and herbs! A sacrilege — to treat foods in this way. Food should be treated with respect, since Our Lord left Himself to us in the guise of food. His disciples knew Him in the breaking of the bread.[2]

Julia Child introduced America to a whole new way of eating in 1961 with her pioneering book *Mastering the Art of French Cooking*. What a contribution she has made! Think of how vegetables were prepared back then and how unacceptable such limp, soggy, and flavorless products would be today. Well into her eighties she guiltlessly favors lots of butter and cream in her preparations, preaching moderation instead of abstinence. The 1997 biography about her was most appropriately entitled *Appetite for Life*. What could be more Christian than to have an appetite for life and a zest for eating? Is not the spiritual opposite, acedia, that listless loss of taste for anything, singled out by spiritual writers as an unmistakable symptom of a soul that is lost?

M. F. K. Fisher is the most acclaimed food writer in recent memory in the United States. Her writings on food have been collected together under the title *The Art of Eating*. Fisher is very down-to-earth, we could say incarnational, when she describes the surprise and the delight that are the aim of her food preparation for guests. But Fisher is also clear that the hunger food satisfies is much more than physical. She explains, "It is impossible to enjoy food without thought. When we exist without thought or thanksgiving for the food we eat, we are not human beings but beasts."[3] In the chapter "An Alphabet for Gourmets," she speaks glowingly of the deeply stirring experience of eating a private meal with just one person, "the peak of contentment, satisfaction, fulfillment, which is a special virtue of sharing food...with one other human being."[4] There are few other moments when we feel so naturally close. Well-prepared food shared by human beings is a natural sacrament of thanksgiving and praise and of communion with other human beings. No wonder Jesus found such a human event wonderfully apt for the Holy Eucharist. When we eat, we are either eating memories or creating them. Jesus understood this when he commanded at the Last Supper, "Do this in memory of me" (Luke 22:19).

The Personal Example of St. Francois

Ste. Jeanne-Francoise describes in her *Testimony* what an indifferent and distracted eater St. Francois was. Sometimes, she said, "he . . . got so absorbed in what he was saying . . . that he quite forgot he was supposed to be eating and drinking, and if he did eat, he didn't give it a thought."[5] She recounts:

> His chief mortification in the matter of food was his attitude of general acceptance without choice, complaint, or criticism. It is certain, and I know it, that he paid little or no attention to what he was eating. One day when he was eating at home with his mother, he was given some poached eggs, still in water as they had been cooked, and people noticed that he was not, in fact, eating the eggs but just dipping his bread in the water and getting on with that. The same thing happened on another occasion when there was some fresh butter floating in the water; for quite a time he went on eating bread dipped in water.[6]

In general, St. Francois tried in the matter of food as in all others to be a good bishop in the style recommended by the reforms of the Council of Trent. Bishops, according to Trent, should have a simple cuisine and be generous in sharing the hospitality of their table with others.

We are told that St. Francois frequently sent uneaten portions of the meals prepared for him to the houses of the poor in his diocese. In these ways he strove to fulfill the biblical injunction, "Be hospitable to one another."

Hospitality holds a central place in the Gospel, as it does in all the great religions of the world. It is always stunning and humbling to be the recipient of the lavish hospitality of a person poorer than yourself; you realize that giving the choicest portions to guests is part of every religious culture. The casualness with which we sometimes treat our guests is perhaps an indicator of how weakened this religious element has become in our culture.

That St. Francois was a diffident eater is well known. What becomes problematical about him, however, with regard to food, is that he refused himself and others any delight in eating. What he says on the subject is so extreme as to make us wonder what is behind such an attitude.

> It is an infallible mark of a wayward, infamous, base, abject, and degraded mind to think about food and drink before mealtime, much more so to delight ourselves later in the pleasure we had in eating, keeping it alive in words and imagination and taking delights in recalling the sensuous satisfaction had in swallowing these bits of food.... People of honor never think of eating except when they sit down at table. After dinner, they wash their hands and mouth so as not to retain the taste or odor of what they have eaten.[7]

The reason for this revulsion toward the enjoyment of food is clearly stated by St. Francois in his *Introduction* — he sees it as a stand-in for sexual pleasure. St. Francois was no Jansenist who found the whole world corrupt and heading for damnation, but the way he discusses food reveals how much he was influenced by the very spiritual tendency he strove to overcome in himself and others. His discussion of food takes place in the context of his teachings about "the sanctity of the marriage bed."

There is a certain resemblance between sexual pleasure and those taken in eating. Both of them are related to the flesh but because of their animal vehemence the first are called carnal pleasures without qualification. I will try to explain what I cannot say about sexual pleasures by what I say of the other.[8]

St. Francois then draws out the resemblance in seven points.

1. The purpose of eating is to maintain life just as the first and principal purpose of sexual relations is to produce children. As such both are a good and holy duty.

2. Beyond the preservation of life, eating and sexual relations are required to maintain mutual intimacy and sharing. St. Paul therefore can describe having sex with one's spouse as a "debt" that is owed to the other (1 Cor. 7:3).

3. Satisfying this "debt" should be done not as if under compulsion but freely and with mutual enjoyment. With regard to sex, even if no children could be foreseen as a consequence, it should still be done with the same freedom and enjoyment.[9]

4. Engaging in eating or sex just for the pleasure of it is not praiseworthy but it is permissible.

5. To be "excessive or inordinate" in gratifying our sensual appetite is worthy of censure.

6. Both eating and sex are fraught with moral danger and can be the source of sin.

After making these points, St. Francois concludes with the final one that we cited above, namely, that it is unworthy of a human being to think about such things beforehand and to try to re-tain their pleasure afterward. St. Francois is keeping in mind the warning of St. Paul not to make a "God of our stomach" (Phil. 3:19).

We may contrast the attitude toward food manifest in Scripture with that of St. Francois. In the life of Jesus the quality and lavishness of the food and drink that Jesus provides are considered indications that these meals are actual anticipations upon earth of what the kingdom of God will be like. Jesus is in a long line of prophets when he connects these meals with the heavenly banquet. Notice how the prophet Isaiah emphasizes how the enjoyment of fine food and drink will be the experience of those who join the Lord upon his holy mountain:

> On this mountain, the Lord of hosts will prepare for all peoples a banquet of rich food, a banquet of fine wines, of food rich and juicy, of fine strained wines. (Isa. 25:6)

Jesus specifically and characteristically directed that the elaborate preparations for his final Passover supper take place and that the ancient food rituals be observed for that meal in which he invested such enormous symbolic value — the institution of the Eucharist (Luke 22:7–13).

Applying the Five Spiritual Principles

We are told if we listen deeply enough to our hearts we will not be led astray. To deny oneself all pleasure in eating and to consider food only a dangerous temptation are symptoms of not listening deeply enough. At a certain level food — and sex — are physical pleasures that, if they become our exclusive preoccupation, can dull us to deeper spiritual satisfactions. But only at a certain level. If we have freed our hearts from slavery to any such compulsion, then they are liberated to celebrate the pleasures of this life as anticipations of the life to come.

The principal means the Christian tradition requires of anyone striving for perfect freedom of heart with regard to food is fasting.

The necessity of prayer and fasting is a constant theme in Scripture (Mark 9:29). With the passing of elaborate rules laying out precisely how one should fast, the practice of fasting itself has unfortunately diminished. This is sometimes justified by the claim that doing something more "positive" like practicing charity is far better. Fasting must once again become a part of our daily living if we are to be true to the Gospel.

If we listen deeply enough to our hearts we will not be led astray.

The *Catechism of the Catholic Church* defines fasting as "refraining from food and drink as an expression of interior penance, in imitation of the fast of Jesus for forty days in the desert."[10] The purpose of fasting as a penitential practice is not a lesser but a greater enjoyment of life. In her book on Christian asceticism, *Fullness of Life*, Margaret Miles stresses that to his followers, Christ is life, greater life. She quotes her mentor, St. Augustine: "I hesitated to die to deadness and live to life."[11] The weight of sinful habits and the deadness that they bring are what penitential practices such as fasting are intended to overcome. She stresses that ascetic practices are directed at what Scripture calls the "flesh," which is quite different from the body or the physical aspect of life. The agenda of the flesh is submission to sex, power, and possessions, the three temptations that Jesus overcame (Matt. 4:1–11). Such an agenda is cruelly hard upon both soul and body. Asceticism therefore brings with it greater energy, freedom, liveliness.[12]

Origen, the early Church Father, helped shape the Christian approach to asceticism. Miles summarizes his teachings as having as their aim "keeping body and soul together." The body, according to Origen, is an accurate reflection of the condition of a person's soul. The body is also the place of the soul's education. Fasting engages our bodies in our religious practice and helps us avoid making our religion something exclusively for our minds.[13]

Some years ago I attended an assembly in Italy of the World Conference of Religions for Peace (W.C.R.P.). It was there that I was introduced to a form of fasting being promoted by a group of Buddhist laypeople, which I have recommended ever since; they called it the "Donate One Meal" program. Once a week you give up one meal and use the time to meditate instead. By meditating you will not be thinking about food. You give the money you save to charity. In this simple practice three values are implemented: empathy, prayer, and service. You develop greater empathy for the poor by feeling hunger yourself. Not eating gives you the freedom to use the time creatively by spending it in prayer. Using the money for charity introduces the dimension of social justice.

St. Francois sees the value of fasting on a regular basis and makes these helpful observations.

1. If you are physically capable of it, set up a routine of fasting on certain days of the week. This will help you control your bodily appetites and grow in virtue as well as gain your heavenly reward.

2. Practice fasting only with the guidance of a good spiritual director and always do so with moderation and balance. Francois quotes St. Jerome approvingly: "Immoderate fasts displease me very much."

3. Your work and state in life are primary; fasting should not impede your ability to perform your duties, or endanger your health. Francois states, "One man finds it difficult to fast, another to take care of the sick, visit prisoners, hear confessions, preach, comfort the afflicted, pray, and perform similar tasks. These last sufferings are of greater value than the first."

4. Eating what is set before you and not criticizing it, whether you like it or not, is itself a great form of asceticism.[14]

Practicing Holiness: The Mass

I once asked someone — no food expert, just a person who likes to cook — why she goes to so much trouble even though frozen and supermarket-prepared foods are so convenient and timesaving. She thought about her answer and mentioned three things. The first is the satisfaction of bringing people together and enjoying their pleasure in eating what you have prepared. In life there are few labors that bring such immediate satisfaction and gratitude as cooking. Then she said, "To cook you have to pay attention." Unless you pay attention, try to achieve the right combinations and temperatures of the ingredients and prepare them carefully, disaster can result. Paying attention is an essential spiritual quality. "Behold," "give ear," "pay attention" were John the Baptist's urgent message in announcing the coming of Christ. Lastly, she said, "You have to be in a good spirit when you set out to cook." Cooking is relaxing for most people. It puts them in a good spirit. It helps them concentrate on something concrete and not be caught up in their own thoughts. In that way, cooking can help a person's religious conversion.

Let us consider the Mass, the heavenly banquet given to us by Christ to enjoy upon earth, with the three reasons offered for the enjoyment of a well-prepared meal.

The Sunday Eucharist is the basic Christian assembly, the weekly gathering of God's people on the first day of the week to recall and celebrate Christ's saving death and glorious Resurrection. The assembly gathers on the first day of the week, the day of the Resurrection, because each Sunday Mass is a "little Easter." The days of the week that follow are to be lived in the spirit and power of the Eucharist with which it began.

> *The Eucharist is to be lived during the coming week by all who have been privileged to share in its celebration in church.*

The cook notes how few times in life we do something that brings immediate expressions of gratitude. In similar fashion the essential attitude we must bring to the Eucharistic celebration must be gratitude: "Let us give thanks to the Lord our God!" The Greek word from which "Eucharist" is derived means "giving thanks." In the Eucharist we give thanks for God's saving deeds on our behalf and ask forgiveness for all our past resentments and transgressions.

"To cook you have to pay attention." To eat the Eucharistic meal also requires sharp attention. "Wisdom! Be attentive!" the deacon admonishes in the Eastern rite before the Word of God is proclaimed. In speaking of "how we must hear the Word of God," St. Francois admonishes, "Always listen to it with attention and reverence; make good use of it; do not let it fall to earth but take it into your heart like a precious balm."[15]

We are more fortunate than St. Francois in having the liturgy celebrated in our own language and in having been given a richer diet of Scripture in the three-year lectionary. But the challenge he lays out remains the same for us as it was for him: we must not only pay attention to but make good use of God's Word. We must take it with us from Mass and strive to live it every day. We recall that the word "Mass" comes from the Latin "missa" and derives from the ancient dismissal of the congregation at its end: "Go, it is sent forth" — "Ite, missa est." What is the "it" that is being sent forth? It is not simply the congregation itself that is now dispersing. It is the Eucharist itself, not only being brought as Holy Communion to those who could not attend Mass, but also the Eucharist as it is to be lived during the coming week by all who have been privileged to share in its celebration in church.

Finally, we are told "a good spirit" is required in the preparation of a fine meal. The guests who participate in such a meal partake of this good spirit. They find themselves more lovingly disposed to one another. In similar fashion St. Francois describes the "intention" we should bring with us every time we come to Mass:

> Your great intention in receiving Communion should be to advance, strengthen, and comfort yourself in the love of God. You must receive with love that which love alone has caused to be given to you. No, you cannot consider our Savior in an action more full of love or more tender than this. In it he abases himself, if we may so express it, and changes himself into food, so that he may penetrate our souls and unite himself most intimately to the heart and body of his faithful.[16]

In the days of St. Francois there raged a controversy about how frequently one should receive Holy Communion. St. Francois invokes St. Augustine's authority in advising that we do so every Sunday, despite our unworthiness. He is quick to point out that we must be free of the awareness of serious transgressions, which otherwise must be confessed and absolved before approaching the

altar. But he feels he must assure married people who have engaged in sexual relations the night before that paying such a "debt"
to one's marriage partner does not disqualify one from receiving
the Eucharist.

St. Francois then goes further and even suggests receiving Holy
Communion every day "with the advice of your spiritual director."[17] If you are challenged as to why you presume to receive
Holy Communion so often, he says you are to tell them "that
it is to learn to love God, be purified from your imperfections,
delivered from misery, comforted in affliction, and supported in
weakness."[18]

For the many who do not have the opportunity, given their
everyday demands, to attend Mass every day, St. Francois offers
an alternative: go to Communion in your heart and in this way,
through a spiritual communion, unite yourself to the life-giving
Body of the Savior.[19]

St. Francois leaves us with this final reflection in his treatment
of the Mass. It is a beautiful illustration of the saying, "You are
what you eat":

> Just as hares in our mountains become white in winter be-
> cause they neither see nor eat anything but snow, so by
> adoring and eating beauty, purity, and goodness itself in this
> divine sacrament you will become wholly beautiful, wholly
> good, and wholly pure.[20]

Ten

Resting

"There is no clock, no matter how good it may be, that doesn't need resetting and rewinding twice a day, once in the morning and once in the evening. In addition, at least once a year, it must be taken apart to remove the dirt clogging it, straighten out bent parts, and repair those worn out."[1]

"Resting" means being in touch on a regular basis with the nourishing and delightful sources of our being. Resting refers to exercising a proper love of ourselves as the foundation of all other loves: as they say, if you have your health, you have everything. Resting, then, means attending to our own hearts and taking proper care of our souls. "Think of yourself first, and then go to others," St. Francois sagely advises.[2]

Resting requires establishing a proper rhythm and balance in our lives. Scripture is filled with warnings about hyperactivity that is really an expression of pride. Neglecting to rest may mean trying to exceed our limits as creatures, trying to be as gods, which is the first or original sin described in the Book of Genesis. Jesus often spoke about the harmful effects of excessive preoccupation with worldly affairs. In his famous saying he warns, "What does it profit a man to gain the whole world and lose his soul in the process?" (Luke 9:25).

If we find ourselves burdened and stressed all the time, we have to ask why. It may be that these burdens are self-imposed and not at all what God is asking of us. Jesus described following him as meaning having our burdens lifted from our shoulders and our spirit lightened. "Come to me, all you who labor and are burdened and I will give you rest. Shoulder my yoke and learn from me, for I am gentle and humble of heart, and you will find rest for your souls. Yes, my yoke is easy and my burden light" (Matt. 11:28–30). If we follow Jesus we will be humble — that is to say, we will respect our human limits and even rejoice in them. We will be gentle with our own spirits and those of others, reducing the high and unrealistic expectations we have of ourselves and of life itself. We will not demand a perfection that we cannot achieve, always being hard on ourselves.

We will explore the importance of observing the Sabbath rest and see what St. Francois advises with regard to rest. The five spiritual principles can work as remedies for anxiety and depression. In the concluding section of this chapter we will lay out a program for an annual retreat as a way of practicing holiness.

The Sabbath Rest

After God freed Israel from slavery in Egypt, God presented Moses, his friend, with the Ten Commandments. These commands are intended to keep us from lapsing again into slavery and to help us preserve our freedom as children of God. The third one is this:

> Remember the Sabbath day and keep it holy. For six days you shall labor and do all your work, but on the seventh day is a sabbath for Yahweh your God. You shall do no work on that day, neither you nor your son nor your daughter nor your servants, men or women, your animals nor the stranger who lives with you. For in six days Yahweh made the heavens

and the earth and the sea and all that these hold, but on
the seventh day he rested: that is why Yahweh has blessed
the Sabbath day and made it sacred. (Exod. 20:8–10)

This command teaches us that there is a huge difference between working in order to live and living in order to work. If we
conceive of life as just working, then we have lost our dignity
as a being made in God's image and likeness and have reduced
ourselves to a beast of burden. If we work in order to live, the
emphasis falls on living, enjoying our life and contemplating our
own goodness and the goodness of all that God has made. Despite
the personal and eternal value of our work, we must lift our eyes
up from our labors on a regular basis and celebrate the beauty and
goodness of God, who blesses our labors and makes them fruitful.

Jesus' parables highlight these truths. In the parable of the
sower, the thorns that choke the growth of the good seed are
said to be "worldly cares" (Luke 8:14) that can invade our souls.
In the parable of the reluctant guests, God gives a party but the
guests refuse to come. The reasons they offer are legitimate: they
have so much else to do that they have no time for a party. They
have excluded themselves from the heavenly wedding feast because they have lost their ability to stop working and celebrate
(Matt. 22:1–14). Our Sabbath rest is all about celebrating life
and its beauty and goodness even in the midst of all the normal
pressures of daily life.

The Teaching of St. Francois on the Need for Rest and Renewal

In describing "resting," St. Francois invokes a variety of attractive
images. He speaks of having our own private space to retreat to
when we need it, and having times of leisure when we can listen to

our hearts.[3] He says we all have the need for solitude, going apart for a while as Jesus invited his disciples to do after they had worked hard (Mark 6:31). Solitude is different from loneliness. Loneliness is being alone unwillingly and disliking it; solitude means being by ourselves because we want to and enjoying its freedom.

St. Francois sees rest as the opportunity to regain perspective and recall all our holy resolutions and good intentions that we tend to forget in daily life. During times of rest and renewal we can use the opportunity to receive the Sacrament of Reconciliation, which will greatly help to heal and restore our spirits.

St. Francois fantasized about retiring to a Swiss mountainside, living in a small chalet, and reading his books. That dream was never realized, but I am sure that just the thought of it brought him great comfort. The times he spent by the lake in Annecy giving spiritual conferences to the nuns must have been for him a much-appreciated release from the pressures of his heavy pastoral duties as a bishop.

Applying the Five Spiritual Principles as Remedies against Anxiety and Depression

One way our hearts tell us we are overburdened and in need of rest is by the twin symptoms of anxiety and depression. We have to take them seriously; unless they are tended to they could undermine our mental and spiritual well-being.

Sometimes the cause of our sadness is an external event over which we have no control: slipping into poverty, becoming sick, losing a friend, or doing something we regret. Other times sadness comes when our minds are confused and our emotions conflicted, when we do not know what we want or what will make us happy even though on the surface everything seems to be going well.

The first piece of advice St. Francois gives is not to increase our anxiety and deepen our depression by trying to make them go away by our own efforts alone. This will only make things worse. Instead we should patiently, meekly, humbly, and calmly "look for deliverance from God who truly loves us and cares for us."[4] In other words, we have to live with these feelings and wait them out. In those dark times our faith will sustain us.

There are, however, some things we can do. We can, St. Francois advises, "take our hearts into our hands," that is to say, not let the feelings of sadness and anxiety simply take over. One positive thing we can do is not to insist on our own timetable for things to be all right. In fact, we should try to be less insistent on having our own way in general and be content with the way things are right now. We can also, by willing it, develop strategies to shut our minds down when they get out of control, not allowing ourselves to be reminded of things that will only get us down.

Another thing we can do, St. Francois suggests, is talk with others. Just trying to put what we feel into words brings relief. Talk with your spiritual director, if you have one, or, if not, with a trusted friend. We might also, even if we do not feel like it, engage in some worthwhile activity, like helping someone else. Just taking the focus off ourselves can change our mood.

Finally, and most importantly, we can pray. To pray is already to do something positive and powerful. Even if we do not feel like praying or question whether our prayers will do any good, we should pray. Turn feelings into prayers; say, "This, Lord, is how it is today."

A classic example of a prayer uttered out of total sadness is Psalm 22. It is the prayer Jesus uttered upon the cross. Some have taken his saying its opening words, "My God, my God, why have you forsaken me?" as a sign of despair. They forget that Jesus no doubt prayed the whole psalm through. Psalm 22 ends with the confident declaration that the pray-er has been heard and will be delivered.

Psalm 22

My God, my God, why have you deserted me?
How far from saving me, the words I groan!
I call all day, my God, but you never answer,
all night long I call and cannot rest.
Yet, Holy One, you
who make your home in the praises of Israel,
in you our fathers put their trust,
they trusted and you rescued them;
they called to you for help and they were saved,
they never trusted you in vain.

Yet here am I, now more worm than man,
scorn of mankind, jest of the people,
all who see me jeer at me,
they toss their heads and sneer,
"He relied on Yahweh, let Yahweh save him!
If Yahweh is his friend, let Him rescue him!"

Yet you drew me out of the womb,
you entrusted me to my mother's breasts;
placed on your lap from my birth,
from my mother's womb you have been my God.
Do not stand aside: trouble is near,
I have no one to help me!

A herd of bulls surrounds me,
strong bulls of Bashan close in on me;
their jaws are agape for me,
like lions tearing and roaring.

I am like water draining away,
my bones are all disjointed,
my heart is like wax,
melting inside me;
my palate is drier than a potsherd
and my tongue is stuck to my jaw.

A pack of dogs surrounds me,
a gang of villains closes me in;
they tie me hand and foot
and leave me lying in the dust of death.

I can count every one of my bones,
and there they glare at me, gloating;
they divide my garments among them
and cast lots for my clothes.

Do not stand aside, Yahweh.
O my strength, come quickly to my help;
rescue my soul from the sword,
my dear life from the paw of the dog,
save me from the lion's mouth,
my poor soul from the wild bulls' horns!

Then I shall proclaim your name to my brothers,
praise you in full assembly:
you who fear Yahweh, praise him!
Entire race of Jacob, glorify him!
Entire race of Israel, revere him!

For he has not despised
or disdained the poor man in his poverty,
has not hidden his face from him,
but has answered him when he called.

You are the theme of my praise in the Great Assembly,
I perform my vows in the presence of those who fear him.
The poor will receive as much as they want to eat.
Those who seek Yahweh will praise him.
Long life to their hearts!

The whole earth, from end to end,
will remember and come back to Yahweh;
all the families of the nations will bow down before him.
For Yahweh reigns, the ruler of nations!
Before him all the prosperous of the earth will bow down,
before him will bow all who go down to the dust.
And my soul will live for him, my children will serve him;
men will proclaim the Lord to generations still to come,
his righteousness to a people yet unborn. All this he has done.

The psalmist expresses the feeling of total abandonment, even by God. Even as he prays he says he feels no one is listening and nothing can help. A small ray of light appears when he recalls that others have placed their trust in God and claimed that this trust was vindicated: "They called to you for help and they were saved, they never trust you in vain" (Ps. 22:5). Even though he himself has no grounds for such trust, the fact that others may have been assisted brings some comfort.

The psalmist then, in his courageous attempt to describe what he is feeling, puts words to his sorrows, his feeling of self-loathing, his sense that people are making fun of him, the fact that he is different. With gripping imagery he describes his symptoms: irrational fears about attacking bulls and lions that threaten him, his feeling of weakness to the point of melting away.

Still feeling no different, he recalls the gift of existence, how he was called out of nothingness by God. Surely, he tries to believe, there must be some purpose to his life that he is not seeing right now. Crossing a threshold, he rises somewhat above his doubt and despair and actually dares to ask for help for his "dear life." In this effort he comes to recognize that God, who made him out of nothing, who cared for him through his human parents when he was young and helpless, will not abandon him now.

Gradually the feeling of isolation begins to recede. He says he now can contemplate rejoining society and even telling everyone how God "has not despised or disdained a poor man in his poverty," that God "has not hidden his face from him but has answered him when he called" (Ps. 22:24).

Psalm 22 is a dramatic exposition of how a life enclosed within itself can, through prayer, open itself up to the grand perspective of God and be freed. "Prayer changes things" is an adage that happens to be true, and the principal thing that prayer changes is the person who is praying.

Through prayer, we are given the ability to reconnect the fragmented pieces of our lives and to experience the peacefulness that comes from the calm possession of ourselves and all our relationships.

Practicing Holiness: The Annual Retreat

In addition to our weekly Sabbath observances and our daily meditation times, we also need opportunities for an annual retreat. Retreat in its religious meaning is an extended time spent apart, often in a retreat house or monastery, where we can "rewind our clocks." Retreats take many forms. Three common kinds are the preached retreat, the guided retreat, and the silent directed retreat. In the past the preached retreat was quite common. A retreat master gave a series of conferences to a group of retreatants who tried to make personal applications of what was said. There are obvious limitations in this "one size fits all" approach. In the guided retreat there are some group conferences, but there is also opportunity for private meetings with the director. The form of retreat most popular today involves no conferences at all, only total silence. The Holy Spirit is the retreat director. What the Spirit discloses is shared daily in a private meeting with the retreat leader. In these meetings the leader often suggests Scripture passages tailored to the needs of the individual retreatant.

The principal thing that prayer changes is the person who is praying.

The topics covered in a retreat are along the lines I call "five easy exercises" taken from St. Francois's *Introduction to the Devout Life*. They center around contemplation of where we are at this particular point in our lives; the progress or lack of progress we are making; the critical relationships we have with God, ourselves, and other people; and, finally, the general state of our hearts.

First Exercise: Preparation

During the first exercise we ponder five beneficial effects that have come into our lives since we entered upon the path of devotion, the changes for the better that we can detect: the ability to stay close to God by regular prayer; the desire to love God above all that we humbly recognize taking root in ourselves; our success in handling troubling passions of the past; the avoidance of so many problems and complications in our lives since we renounced sin; and, finally, the frequency of our access to the sacraments, especially Holy Communion. Be thankful for all these. Let us bless God and praise God for them from the depths of our hearts.

Second Exercise: God

The second exercise is centered upon the primary relationship with God. St. Francois urges that we begin this exercise by inventorying our life to see if we are free of the disfiguring effects of mortal sin. As we try to obey God's commandments more faithfully over a long period of time, we should find them easier and more congenial, rather than more difficult to observe, since they are leading us upon a path of greater personal fulfillment and happiness. Are we continuing to be aware of lesser faults and failings and trying to eliminate these as well?

Our personal rule of life is a good measuring stick for this exercise. St. Francois mentions specifically our fidelity to attending to God's Word in Scripture and our regular meditation upon it as the means to our continuing conversion. He also calls attention to the regularity of confession, spiritual direction, and participation in the Eucharist.

Is God as close to us as we would like? Do we find ourselves thinking about God apart from regular prayer times and when we are doing other things? God becomes especially real and comes close to us in the person of Jesus, the perfect revelation of the Father. Are we finding refreshment and joy in our companionship with Jesus, knowing his love for us, his infinite patience and compassion for our weaknesses, the limitless depths of his mercy and forgiveness?

Devotion to Mary the Mother of God and to the saints and angels is closely related to our love of Jesus. Devotion to them gives warmth and density to our love of God as we feel their constant support.

Our relationship with God must show itself in the good fruits of how we live. If God has become our true priority we are willing to sacrifice other, lesser things. In this exercise we should ponder what specific differences we can detect in the ways we live that manifest this supreme commitment.

Third Exercise: Ourselves

In this exercise we pay attention to our own lives — our spiritual, physical, and emotional good health. We ask ourselves if our lives in general are well ordered or out of control. Are our priorities the right ones? On the spiritual side, do we strive to make God and God's will for us our first priority? Is God's evaluation of us more important than what anyone else thinks of us? In our emotional lives, do we have a proper estimation of our own value as people, of our strengths and weaknesses? It is not against Christian humility to have a proper regard for ourselves; what is against humility is to measure our personal worth in comparison with other people, thinking ourselves lesser or greater than they are. Am I taking good care of my body by doing regular exercise, eating properly, and getting enough sleep?

Fourth Exercise: Our Relationships

In this fourth exercise, which allows us to turn a critical eye upon our human relationships, St. Francois directs our attention first to the most central relationships, those involving people with whom we enjoy special bonds: our families and close friends. These relationships must be cultivated and carefully attended to lest they weaken or wither. He also speaks in the second place about other relationships, especially those involving difficult people whom we have to deal with. Is the problem with ourselves? he asks. Are we really well disposed toward them?

Forgiveness of injuries at the hands of others is fundamental to the Gospel way of living. Love of enemies displays the quality of love better than love of friends. In trying to mend tattered human relationships, we should keep in mind the immense patience of

God, who does not demand instant change but allows wheat and weeds to grow up together lest more harm than good be done (Matt. 13:24–30).

Fifth Exercise: An Examination of Consciousness

In this final exercise we are to consider the state of our heart in general. The previous exercises are intended to lead to this overall review of our condition. Spiritual directors call this kind of review an "examination of consciousness" as opposed to an "examination of conscience." St. Francois makes this same distinction without using these precise terms. An examination of conscience, he explains, refers only to our sins, which we need to inventory before presenting them for absolution in the sacrament of penance. This simple avoidance of sin and seeking forgiveness for sins committed is, he says, for those who have no thought of advancement in devotion. The examination of consciousness, on the other hand — what St. Francois calls the consideration "of the state of our heart" — is for those who have embarked upon the path of devotion and need to assess the degree of progress they are making.

What affections, not necessarily sinful ones, continue to entangle our heart? What passions still hold our heart in their grip? To do this fine tuning, we have to consider our present loves, dislikes, desires, hopes, sadness, and joys. Are our lives in proper order? Do we still find ourselves desiring wealth, pleasure, honors? What are we still afraid of? What continues to make us sad? What drives and motivates us? Is it something spiritual, or something less honorable?

The fifth part of the *Introduction to the Devout Life* concludes with some thoughts that we should keep in mind at all times in order to remain faithful to our resolution to pursue the way of devotion:

How beautifully made I am as coming from the hand of God.

How delightful and how fitting for me is the virtuous life.

How many are the good people who inspire me.

How much Jesus has shown his love for me.

How fortunate I am to hear God say to me, "I have loved you with an everlasting love — therefore I have drawn you to me and made you mine."

Because of its ambitious agenda, a retreat like the one described here is best done with the aid of a director. Even if we do not have access to a retreat house and a retreat master, we do not need to deprive ourselves of the retreat experience. Time away to do spiritual work can be found in a variety of ways and places. What is essential is that we make a retreat on a regular basis for the sake of our souls and bodies.

Conclusion

Every spiritual method ought to be judged by its results. The method we have presented here as grounded in the five spiritual principles has proven itself to be extraordinarily fruitful in the lives of many people. By way of conclusion we cite the example of one holy person who recently was given official recognition by the Church, Blessed John XXIII.

In the case of Pope John — who was born Angelo Roncalli in a small town, Sotto il Monte, in northern Italy — we are fortunate to have an extraordinary record of his spiritual strivings. From the age of fourteen until six months before his death, Pope John kept a spiritual journal, which was published after his death. The underlying theme of *Journal of a Soul* is Pope John's cultivation of personal humility. Humility in his case means not always following one's own desires and plans but subsuming one's desires to the great designs of God. "This is the mystery of my life," he writes; "do not look for other explanations."[1] This is also the central insight of the spirituality of St. Francois de Sales that guided Pope John throughout his life. "Where there is less of my will there is more of God's" was how St. Francois expressed it. John's prayer, which surely was realized in his life, was simply, "Let everything in us be on a grand scale."[2]

During four of the five years of his pontificate I was a seminarian in Rome. Observing him up close as I did, I saw that as pope he continued to be simply himself, no small spiritual achievement.

John XXIII: Salesian Saint

Like many others, the philosopher Hannah Arendt, colleague of Martin Heidegger and Karl Jaspers, was swept up in admiration of Pope John XXIII. Her review of *Journal of a Soul* when it appeared was entitled "Angelo Guiseppe Roncalli: A Christian on St. Peter's Chair." She says with astonishment, "In the midst of our century this man had decided to take literally, and not symbolically, every article of faith he had ever been taught. He really wanted 'to be crushed, despised, neglected for the love of Jesus.' "[3] She admired what she described as his "complete independence which comes from a true detachment from the things of this world, the splendid freedom from prejudice and convention."[4] She attributes his self-confidence to the ability he had of treating everybody, high and low, as his equal. The colorful anecdotes and stories that assembled around him demonstrated his conviction that the everyday language of the pope need not be full of mystery and awe. But she has to admit she found *Journal of a Soul* both "strangely disappointing and strangely fascinating."[5]

Her reasons for this are illuminating in terms of John's spirituality as it is revealed in *Journal of a Soul*. She says, "Written for the most part in periods of retreat, it consists of endlessly repetitive devout outpourings and self-exhortations, 'examinations of conscience' and notations of 'spiritual progress,' with only the rarest references to actual happenings, so that for pages and pages it reads like an elementary textbook on how to be good and avoid evil."[6] In other words, *Journal of a Soul* is a perfect example of the devout life as described in St. Francois's *Introduction to the Devout Life* by someone who actually lived it all his life. In addition to regular retreats and daily examinations of conscience, as Arendt points out, there is recorded there his fidelity to a personal rule of life, spiritual reading, frequent confession, and spiritual direction.

Arendt expresses her greatest disappointment with *Journal of a Soul* that its author, who broke frontiers in the reform and renewal of the Church, never noted even the few instances she could trace of intellectual development. It should be said in reply that the effects of John's reforms on the Church and world, their radicalness, came not because John took an intellectual approach to the problems facing the Church but because he obeyed and boldly implemented the spiritual insights that he had carefully cultivated over many years.

> **"I must desire, not to be what I am not, but to be very truly what I really am."**

It would be incorrect to say that St. Francois de Sales was the only spiritual source Blessed John XXIII drew upon. Surely the *Imitation of Christ* and the writings of the English priest Frederick Faber would have to be high on the list. But woven through *Journal of a Soul* is the personal appropriation of meekness, humility, and kindness, a holy indifference with regard to worldly things and events, and a complete openness to the will of God, all hallmarks of Salesian spirituality.

But the key insight that John derived from St. Francois and the one that had the most pervasive influence on his entire life was one he noted in *Journal of a Soul* when he was twenty-one years old and in the seminary in Rome. John wrote: "I must desire, not to be what I am not, but to be very truly what I really am. That is what my St. Francois de Sales tells me."[7] He elaborates upon this critical spiritual turning point in a later entry:

Practical experience has now convinced me of this: the concept of holiness which I had formed and applied to myself was mistaken. In every one of my actions, and in the little failings of which I was immediately aware, I used to call to mind the image of some saint whom I had set myself to imitate down to the smallest particular, as a painter makes an exact copy of a picture by Raphael. I used to say to myself: in this case St. Aloysius would have done so and so, or: he would not do this or that. However, it turned out that I was never able to achieve what I had thought I could do, and this worried me. The method was wrong. From the saints I must take the substance, not the accidents, of their virtues. I am not St. Aloysius, nor must I seek holiness in this particular way, but according to the requirements of my own nature, my own character, and the different conditions of my life. I must not be the dry, bloodless reproduction of a model, however perfect. God desires us to follow the examples of the saints by absorbing the vital sap of their virtues and turning it into our own life-blood, adapting it to our individual capacities and particular circumstances. If St. Aloysius had been as I am, he would have become holy in a different way.[8]

John had absorbed well the concept of the devout life that St. Francois elaborated — that there is no one way to live the devout life; it is to be practiced by each of us out of our own personality, temperament, vocation, state in life, health, and other particular circumstances. Moreover, all these ways of devotion are equally valid and meritorious. This Salesian insight freed John — even when he assumed the august position of successor of St. Peter and vicar of Christ — simply to be himself. He could do this because the highest calling of all, the baptismal calling to be a follower of Christ, was to be no more or less than who we are in the eyes of God.

How amazing it is, as we reflect upon it, that the same Baroque spirituality that shaped St. Francois de Sales and Ste. Jeanne-Francoise de Chantal, and which, in turn, was shaped by them, should remain in full vigor in our own age and produce a saint such as Blessed John XXIII three hundred years later.

There are ways in which this spiritual tradition needs to be modified and expanded, and I have indicated some of them. But we will continue to draw from and be inspired by this spirituality long into the future, just as we continue to thrill to the sublime music of Bach, Palestrina, Vivaldi, Handel, and Mozart.

Belonging to God as a Way of Life

The great task of any Christian, as has often been said, is "becoming who you are." As God's own sons and daughters, baptized into the image of Jesus, we seek more and more to belong totally to God and to remove any inconsistencies that get in the way. The goal of the spiritual life, it is said, is for the heavenly Father, gazing upon Jesus and ourselves, not to be able to tell us apart.

We seek only to know God's will for us, the personal calling that will reveal the mysterious design of the life God meant for us in which will lie our happiness. John XXIII's personal motto was "Obedientia et pax," "Obedience and peace." Peace comes from obeying God's will, not our own.

In the *mystagogia* period of Christian Initiation, newly received members of the Church, like Steve, strive to take in and grasp the abundant grace that has been given them in Baptism, Confirmation, and the Holy Eucharist. For all Christians, including those like Aaron who were baptized at birth, the spiritual breakthrough comes when we realize that our religion can become personal, something that is part of who we are, that defines us. Out of this realization we become aware that our lives have been invested with a great purpose that only we can accomplish.

St. Francois de Sales has taught us not to let our personal limitations and failings discourage us or make us not believe in our sublime calling. John XXIII, as his journal makes clear, tried many times, for example, to moderate his eating habits and control his weight; he never succeeded. St. Francois preached moderation and balance between prayer and activity but never perfectly achieved these himself. This is all part of living the life of holiness. Holiness means belonging to God, not just moral goodness and perfection. We never give up trying to be good because we know we are God's own: this is our perfection and our holiness. We know to whom we belong, St. Paul said, despite our many weaknesses (2 Cor. 10:7).

Some Suggestions for Further Personal Reflection

One / Five Spiritual Principles for Beginners

~ What are some ways I can listen more deeply to my own heart and hear what it is telling me?

~ How can I be gentler with my own spirit as well as with the spirits of others?

Two / Seeking a Spiritual Guide

~ Where would I go to find the spiritual guidance I need to make progress in the spiritual life?

~ What would I identify as my own greatest failing and the corresponding virtue I need to cultivate to overcome it?

Three / Developing a Personal Rule of Life

~ In what ways can I detect that my spiritual life is off course and what do I have to do to give my life more balance and satisfaction?

~ Taking into account obligations and circumstances I cannot change, what are the things at the end of each day that I would be greatly disappointed I had not fitted in because they really nourish me?

Four / The Goal of the Spiritual Life:
Falling in Love with God

~ How would I describe at this time my personal relationship with God? Can I recall a time when I felt especially close to God or that God actually spoke to me?

~ Many things belong to me, but to whom or what do I belong?

Five / Changing

~ If even after much trying I cannot remove all the inconsistencies and imperfections in my life, how can I, like St. Augustine, learn to live more comfortably with myself and my own humanity?

~ How can I develop the patience to be satisfied with little changes, realizing that progress in the spiritual life is usually "little by little" or often undetectable?

Six / Praying

~ Jesus tells us to "pray always" (Luke 18:1). How is this to be done?

~ Reading the Scriptures daily and pondering them in my heart is a road to deeper conversion. With the help of the Church's Lectionary, can I read over each day's Scripture passages before retiring and then find time in the morning to access the insights given me even while I was asleep?

Seven / Loving

~ St. Francois in his spirituality lays great emphasis upon the practice of the so-called "small virtues" as the way of exercising divine charity. What would I identify as small virtues that I can cultivate?

~ Why, in the end, are they really not so "small"?

Eight / Working

~ What are some of the ways I can go to work each day and not, as it is said, "leave my soul in the parking lot"?

~ What can I do within my sphere of influence to bring the Kingdom of God to that place?

Nine / Eating

~ In what ways can an ordinary and necessary activity such as eating become a spiritual experience?

~ How can I "go to Communion in my heart" outside of Mass, uniting myself with the life-giving Body of my Savior?

Ten / Resting

~ At Mass we pray that we may be released from useless anxiety and live our lives with joyful hope. What does paying attention to my need for rest and recreation contribute to living my life with more joy and hope?

~ St. Francois, Ste. Jeanne-Francoise, and Blessed John XXIII are rightly revered as hope persons, yet each in significant ways failed to achieve at all times the perfection they were seeking. What does this say about my not being discouraged with myself for not achieving all of my own spiritual goals?

Notes

Introduction

1. St. Francois de Sales, *Introduction to the Devout Life,* translated and edited by John K. Ryan (New York: Doubleday Image Books, 1989), 44.

2. St. Francois de Sales, *Introduction to the Devout Life,* 40.

3. St. Francois de Sales, *Introduction to the Devout Life,* 44.

4. *Lumen Gentium: Constitution on the Church,* in *The Documents of Vatican II,* edited by Walter M. Abbott, S.J. (New York: Crossroad, 1989), 40–41.

5. Rudolf Otto, in his classic work *The Idea of the Holy,* explains that the word "holy" belongs to the sphere of religion, our relatedness to God. Holiness in the sense of moral goodness pertains to the realm of ethics. Rudolf Otto, *The Idea of the Holy,* translated by John W. Harvey (New York: Oxford, 1958), 5–6.

6. St. Francois de Sales, *Introduction to the Devout Life,* 41.

7. *Lumen Gentium,* 40–41.

8. St. Francois de Sales, *Introduction to the Devout Life,* 43–44.

9. Pope John Paul II, *Novo Millennio Ineunte* (January 6, 2001), *Origins* 30, no. 31 (January 18, 2001).

10. St. Francois de Sales, *Introduction to the Devout Life,* 40–41

One / Five Spiritual Principles for Beginners

1. Michael de la Bedoyère, *Saint Maker: The Remarkable Life of St. Francis de Sales, Shepherd of Kings and Commoners, Sinners and Saints* (Manchester: Sophia Institute, 1998), 8.

2. *St. Francis de Sales: A Testimony by St. Chantal,* translated and edited by Elizabeth Stopp (Hyattsville, Md.: Institute of Salesian Studies, 1967), 170.

3. Henri Brémond, *A Literary History of Religious Thought in France from the Wars of Religion Down to Our Times,* translated by K. L. Montgomery (New York: Macmillan, 1928), 1:57–58.

4. *Oeuvres de Saint Francois de Sales, évèque de Génève et docteur de l'église,* 27 vols., Annecy edition, 1892, XIII, 330. Translations are by the author.

5. St. Francois de Sales, *Introduction to the Devout Life,* 127.

6. Cited by Elizabeth Stopp, *A Man to Heal Differences: Essays and Talks on St. Francis de Sales* (Philadelphia: St. Joseph's University, 1997), 181.

7. See *Oeuvres de Saint Francois de Sales,* XII, 173, for an example.

8. St. Francis de Sales, *Treatise on the Love of God*, translated by Dom Henry Bernard Mackey, O.S.B. (Rockford, Ill.: Tan, 1997), 57–58.

9. *The Confessions of St. Augustine*, translated by John K. Ryan (New York: Doubleday Image, 1960), 227.

10. Henri de Lubac, S.J., *Augustinianism and Modern Theology* (New York: Crossroad, 2000), 179.

11. St. Francois de Sales, *Introduction to the Devout Life*, 42.

12. St. Francois de Sales, *Introduction to the Devout Life*, 51.

13. St. Francois de Sales, *Introduction to the Devout Life*, 88.

14. St. Francois de Sales, *Introduction to the Devout Life*, 68.

15. St. Francois de Sales, *Introduction to the Devout Life*, 162.

16. St. Francois de Sales, *Introduction to the Devout Life*, 162.

17. *St. Francois de Sales: A Testimony by St. Chantal*, 64–65.

18. *St. Francois de Sales: A Testimony by St. Chantal*, 168.

19. *St. Francois de Sales: A Testimony by St. Chantal*, 81.

20. *Oeuvres de Saint Francois de Sales*, XIII, 289–92.

21. *Live Jesus! Wisdom from St. Francis de Sales and St. Jane de Chantal* (Jamesville, Md.: The Word Among Us, 2000), 52.

22. Francis de Sales, *Finding God Where You Are: Selected Spiritual Writings*, edited by Joseph F. Power, O.S.F.S. (Hyde Park, N.Y.: New City, 1993), 25.

23. St. Francis de Sales, *Treatise on the Love of God*, 540–41.

24. St. Francois de Sales, *Introduction to the Devout Life*, 121–22.

Two / Seeking a Spiritual Guide

1. St. Francois de Sales, *Introduction to the Devout Life*, 45.

2. St. Francois de Sales, *Introduction to the Devout Life*, 47.

3. St. Francois de Sales, *Introduction to the Devout Life*, 47.

4. St. Francois de Sales, *Introduction to the Devout Life*, 46.

5. *St. Francois de Sales: A Testimony by St. Chantal*, 119–20.

6. St. Francois de Sales, *Introduction to the Devout Life*, 184.

7. St. Irenaeus, *Against Heresies*, as cited by Margaret R. Miles in *Fullness of Life: Historical Foundations for a New Asceticism* (Philadelphia: Westminster Press, 1981), 30.

8. St. Francois de Sales, *Introduction to the Devout Life*, 94.

9. St. Francois de Sales, *Introduction to the Devout Life*, 280.

10. St. Francois de Sales, *Introduction to the Devout Life*, 280.

11. *St. Francois de Sales: A Testimony by St. Chantal*, 108.

12. *Oeuvres de Saint Francois de Sales*, XIV, 1–3.

13. St. Francois de Sales, *Introduction to the Devout Life*, 146.

14. St. Francois de Sales, *Introduction to the Devout Life*, 148.

15. St. Francois de Sales, *Introduction to the Devout Life*, 149.

16. St. Francois de Sales, *Introduction to the Devout Life*, 139.

17. St. Francois de Sales, *Introduction to the Devout Life*, 140.

18. St. Francois de Sales, *Introduction to the Devout Life*, 141.

19. St. Francois de Sales, *Introduction to the Devout Life*, 147.

20. St. Francois de Sales, *Introduction to the Devout Life*, 148.

21. Wendy Wright, *Francis de Sales: Introduction to the Devout Life and Treatise on the Love of God* (New York: Crossroad, 1997), 26.

22. *St. Francois de Sales: A Testimony by St. Chantal*, 169.

Three / Developing a Personal Rule of Life

1. *The Confessions of St. Augustine*, 278.

2. St. Francois de Sales, *Introduction to the Devout Life*, 93–119.

3. Wendy Wright, *Bond of Perfection: Jeanne de Chantal and Francois de Sales* (Mahwah, N.J.: Paulist Press, 1985), 133.

4. *Oeuvres de Saint Francois de Sales*, XIII, 318.

5. de la Bedoyère, *Saint Maker*, 214.

6. *St. Francois de Sales: A Testimony by St. Chantal*, 166.

7. *St. Francois de Sales: A Testimony by St. Chantal*, 167.

8. Benedict J. Groeschel, C.F.R., and Terrence L. Webber, *Thy Will Be Done: A Spiritual Portrait of Terence Cardinal Cooke* (New York: Alba House, 1990), 55.

9. John Henry Newman, "A Short Road to Perfection" (September 27, 1856), *Prayers, Verses and Devotions* (San Francisco: Ignatius, 1989), 328.

10. "A Short Road to Perfection," 329.

Four / The Goal of the Spiritual Life

1. St. Margaret Mary Alacoque, *The Autobiography*, translated by the Sisters of the Visitation (Rockford, Ill.: Tan, 1986), 88.

2. St. Margaret Mary Alacoque, *The Autobiography*, 76.

3. St. Margaret Mary Alacoque, *The Autobiography*, 39.

4. St. Margaret Mary Alacoque, *The Autobiography*, 76.

Five / Changing

1. St. Francois de Sales, *Introduction to the Devout Life*, 48.

2. St. Francois de Sales, *Introduction to the Devout Life*, 39–40.

3. *The Confessions of St. Augustine*, 43.

4. *The Confessions of St. Augustine*, 104.

5. St. Francois de Sales, *Introduction to the Devout Life*, 41.

6. St. Francois de Sales, *Introduction to the Devout Life*, 40.

7. *The Confessions of St. Augustine*, 233.

8. *The Confessions of St. Augustine*, 133.

9. *The Confessions of St. Augustine*, 202.

10. W. W. Meissner, S.J., M.D., *Ignatius of Loyola: The Psychology of a Saint* (New Haven, Conn.: Yale University Press, 1992), 176.

11. *The Confessions of St. Augustine*, 45.

12. St. Francois de Sales, *Introduction to the Devout Life*, 47–48.

13. *The Confessions of St. Augustine*, 50.

Six / Praying

1. St. Francois de Sales, *Introduction to the Devout Life*, 84–85.

2. *St. Francois de Sales: A Testimony by St. Chantal*, 166–67.

3. St. Francois de Sales, *Introduction to the Devout Life*, 93.

4. St. Francois de Sales, *Introduction to the Devout Life*, 84.

5. St. Teresa of Jesus, *The Book of Her Life*, 8, 5, in *The Collected Works of St. Teresa of Avila*, translated by Kieran Kavanaugh, O.C.D., and Otilio Rodriguez, O.C.D. (Washington, D.C.: Institute of Carmelite Studies, 1976), I, 67.

6. Cathleen Medwick, *Teresa of Avila: The Progress of a Soul* (New York: Alfred A. Knopf, 1999), 137.

7. St. Francois de Sales, *Introduction to the Devout Life*, 34.

8. St. Francois de Sales, *Introduction to the Devout Life*, 91.

9. St. Francois de Sales, *Introduction to the Devout Life*, 103.

10. Mariano Magrassi, *Praying the Bible: An Introduction to Lectio Divina* (Collegeville, Minn.: Liturgical Press, 1988), 6.

Seven / Loving

1. St. Francois de Sales, *Introduction to the Devout Life*, 121.

2. *St. Francois de Sales: A Testimony by St. Chantal*, 170.

3. *The Confessions of St. Augustine*, 206.

4. *Oeuvres de Saint Francois de Sales*, XVII, 190, "He has made us one heart."

5. *Oeuvres de Saint Francois de Sales*, XII, 262.

6. *Oeuvres de Saint Francois de Sales*, XII, 263.

7. *Oeuvres de Saint Francois de Sales*, XII, 321.

8. *Oeuvres de Saint Francois de Sales*, XII, 285.

9. St. Francis de Sales, *Treatise on the Love of God*, 428.

10. *The Confessions of St. Augustine*, 155.

11. *The Confessions of St. Augustine*, 100.

12. *The Confessions of St. Augustine*, 65–66.

13. *Oeuvres de Saint Francois de Sales*, XVII, 216–17.

14. Cited by Wright, *Bond of Perfection*, 168.

15. Wright, *Bond of Perfection*, 187.

16. Wright, *Bond of Perfection*, 187.

17. *St. Francois de Sales: A Testimony by St. Chantal*, 147.

18. *St. Francois de Sales: A Testimony by St. Chantal*, 152.

19. *St. Francois de Sales: A Testimony by St. Chantal,* 64.
20. Brémond, *A Literary History of Religious Thought in France,* 394.
21. St. Francois de Sales, *Introduction to the Devout Life,* 122.
22. St. Francois de Sales, *Introduction to the Devout Life,* 124.
23. St. Francois de Sales, *Introduction to the Devout Life,* 123.
24. St. Francois de Sales, *Introduction to the Devout Life,* 130.

Eight / Working

1. St. Francois de Sales, *Introduction to the Devout Life,* 153.
2. Vatican Council II, *Gaudium et Spes: The Church in the Modern World,* 39, 43.
3. *St. Francois de Sales: A Testimony by St. Chantal,* 131.
4. *St. Francois de Sales: A Testimony by St. Chantal,* 55.
5. *St. Francois de Sales: A Testimony by St. Chantal,* 67.
6. *St. Francois de Sales: A Testimony by St. Chantal,* 167.

Nine / Eating

1. St. Francois de Sales, *Introduction to the Devout Life,* 103.
2. Dorothy Day, *By Little and by Little: The Selected Writings of Dorothy Day,* edited by Robert Ellsberg (New York: Alfred A. Knopf, 1983), 361.
3. M. F. K. Fisher, *The Art of Eating* (New York: Macmillan, 1990), xv.
4. Fisher, *The Art of Eating,* 743.
5. *St. Francois de Sales: A Testimony by St. Chantal,* 80.
6. *St. Francois de Sales: A Testimony by St. Chantal,* 79.
7. St. Francois de Sales, *Introduction to the Devout Life,* 228.
8. St. Francois de Sales, *Introduction to the Devout Life,* 226.
9. An example is the case envisioned by Pope Paul VI in *Humanae Vitae* ("Of Human Life") 16: "Certainly there may be serious reasons for spacing offspring. These may be based on the physical or psychological condition of the spouses or on external factors. The Church teaches that in such cases it is morally permissible for spouses to calculate their fertility by observing the natural rhythms inherent in the generative faculties and to reserve marital intercourse for infertile times."
10. *Catechism of the Catholic Church* (Washington, D.C.: United States Catholic Conference, Libreria Editrice Vaticana, 1994), 879.
11. *The Confessions of St. Augustine,* 189.
12. Margaret R. Miles, *Fullness of Life: Historical Foundations for a New Asceticism* (Philadelphia: Westminster, 1981), 158.
13. Miles, *Fullness of Life,* 58.
14. St. Francois de Sales, *Introduction to the Devout Life,* 185–86.
15. St. Francois de Sales, *Introduction to the Devout Life,* 108.
16. St. Francois de Sales, *Introduction to the Devout Life,* 118.

17. St. Francois de Sales, *Introduction to the Devout Life*, 117.
18. St. Francois de Sales, *Introduction to the Devout Life*, 118.
19. St. Francois de Sales, *Introduction to the Devout Life*, 118.
20. St. Francois de Sales, *Introduction to the Devout Life*, 119.

Ten / Resting

1. St. Francois de Sales, *Introduction to the Devout Life*, 271.
2. St. Francois de Sales, *Introduction to the Devout Life*, 189.
3. St. Francois de Sales, *Introduction to the Devout Life*, 371.
4. St. Francois de Sales, *Introduction to the Devout Life*, 251.

Conclusion

1. Pope John XXIII, *Journal of a Soul*, translated by Dorothy White (New York: McGraw-Hill, 1965), 326.
2. Pope John XXIII, *Journal of a Soul*, 397.
3. Hannah Arendt, *Men in Dark Times* (New York: Harcourt, Brace & World, 1968), 60.
4. Arendt, *Men in Dark Times*, 57.
5. Arendt, *Men in Dark Times*, 57.
6. Arendt, *Men in Dark Times*, 57.
7. Pope John XXIII, *Journal of a Soul*, 95.
8. Pope John XXIII, *Journal of a Soul*, 106–7.

About the Author

It is an honor for Crossroad to present this book. When we first read it, the prose stayed with us the way a lovely melody stays in one's mind. The goal of this book is to give people a glimpse into the power of solid spiritual direction, in order to see ourselves more clearly and help us grow as lovers of God. By presenting these ideas in such a direct and clear way, Msgr. Murphy gives us a taste of the path he is inviting us to take — if we read thoughtfully, we are already on our way.

This book represents the culmination of a long career as writer and teacher. Murphy holds a doctorate from the Gregorian University and served as rector at the North American College in Vatican City. He is presently pastor of the Holy Martyrs Parish in Falmouth, Maine. His previous books include *At Home on Earth: Foundations for a Catholic Ethic of the Environment* (with Crossroad), and *Wallace Stevens: A Spiritual Poet in a Secular Age.* He currently lives in Falmouth, Maine, which seems a location well-suited to Murphy's lyric sensibilities and respect for the environment.

As we gave the manuscript to others to read, they invariably replied, "I wish Monsignor Murphy could be *my* spiritual director." With this book, their wish is fulfilled.